i·ching life

BECOMING YOUR
AUTHENTIC SELF

i·ching life

Becoming Your Authentic Self

NEW REVISED EDITION

BY WU WEI

POWER PRESS
LOS ANGELES, CALIFORNIA

Library of Congress Control Number: 2006930175

ISBN: 0-943015-52-9

New Revised Edition 10 9 8 7 6 5 4 3 2 1

For information, address:
        Power Press
        6428 Meadows Court
        Malibu, California 90265
        Telephone: 310/392-9393
        E-mail: wuwei@power-press.com
        Website: www.power-press.com

Cover design: Roger Gefvert
Interior art by Wu Wei

The symbol on the title page is the Chinese word picture for change. It was
painted with five quick slashes of Wu Wei's ink brush.

For you, my companion,
who is traveling with me through
space and time, inside the consciousness
that is the Universe, on our way to a destination
yet to be known, just existing, just experiencing,
just being a part of It all. How glorious!
What an honor!

Wu Wei

Contents

Preface

The information in this book has been set forth with one goal: to enable you to enjoy a better, fuller, easier, more productive life, free from the pitfalls that may have earlier beset your path. It is a guide, showing you the way to be what the I Ching describes as "a superior person" and suggesting ways to use the I Ching to accomplish that goal and others you desire.

Why should you want to follow the life of a superior person? Because of the law of cause and effect, which states: "Every action produces a result, and the result is in perfect accord with the action." Therefore, if you live the life of a superior person, meaning a person of worthy motives who always strives to be the best he can be, you will naturally achieve a life of peaceful harmony, having what you want and being who you want. Your path will be straight, the wind will be fair, the sun will shine upon you, and your progress will be as an eagle in full flight.

I have written a book called *I Ching Wisdom: Guidance*

from the Book of Answers, which sets forth some of the volatile sayings from the I Ching. I use the word *volatile* because one the meanings of volatile is "having the power to fly." These volatile sayings from the I Ching will give you the power to fly, will give you the power to break loose from that which has held you back, will empower you to reach lofty goals, will provide the means for you to soar to the heights of success, and will show you how to avoid the pitfalls that beset the path of the unenlightened.

In *I Ching Wisdom*, after each saying I have written a comment that expands the meaning of the saying to help readers grasp the wisdom contained within the saying. The sayings in *I Ching Wisdom* demonstrate the function of Universal laws, and because they elaborate certain basic concepts in *I Ching Life*, I have incorporated some of those sayings and comments into this book. This serves a twofold purpose: one, to further clarify the concepts in this book, and two, to further expand on the meanings of the sayings in *I Ching Wisdom*. You will see those sayings from the I Ching set off throughout this book.

The I Ching teaches:

Knowledge
is the key to freedom.

Knowledge comes in many forms. Knowing how to earn a living frees you from poverty. Knowing how to keep healthy frees you from sickness. Knowing how to entertain yourself frees you from boredom. And knowing the path of the superior person frees you from misfortune, failure, and suffering.

The knowledge that you will gain from living life according to I Ching precepts is knowledge that is coming to you from across the span of thousands of years. It is the knowledge that has been carried to you in a direct line from Fu Hsi, the great Chinese sage who created the I Ching. That knowledge has sustained your predecessors, sustained their very lives, and carried them to the greatest heights attainable in world affairs and personal life. Emperors and common folk alike who have possessed this knowledge have savored the best that life has to offer and have gone their ways fulfilled and happy, content as a puppy after drinking his fill of his mother's warm, nourishing milk.

AUTHOR'S APOLOGY TO WOMEN READERS

I sincerely apologize for using *he*, *his*, *him* when speaking generally. Using *he/she* throughout becomes cumbersome for the reader and disturbs the flow of thought. I chose to use the masculine form because it is what we are accustomed to seeing in print and because the goal is to make the reading easy.

Wu Wei

AUTHOR'S APOLOGY TO ALL READERS

I humbly apologize to you for my presumption that I know something that you do not and for my egotistical assumption that I know anything at all. All information comes from one source, the Universe, and since we are all part of it, its information belongs to us all and is available to each of us. On the small chance that I have spent more time seeking out information about the I Ching and ways to use it than you have and therefore may have received information which you may not have yet received, and because I want you to have as much information as possible about the I Ching, I risk this great presumption. Please overlook and forgive my immodesty. That I undertake this work at all is only because of my love for the great wisdom and my sincere desire to impart it to you.

Your humble and insignificant servant,

AUTHOR'S NOTES

The concept upon which this book is based is that the Universe is alive, conscious, and aware. By using the I Ching, we can communicate with the Universal Intelligence of which we are a part and which will guide us to better, fuller lives, filled with abundance and well-being. That we can control our destinies and that we can, by taking the appropriate action, enjoy a lifetime of great good fortune and supreme success are the basic assumptions upon which this book is written.

I strongly recommend the use of yarrow stalks in conjunction with I Ching divination. All other methods of divination using the I Ching are, at best, poor substitutes for the use of yarrow stalks, the original method. I have given complete instructions on how to use yarrow stalks in my books *The I Ching: The Book of Answers* and *The I Ching Workbook*, published by Power Press. Yarrow stalks are also available through the publisher (see copyright page or the products page at the end of the book for more information).

In this book, the word *Universe* is capitalized to acknowledge its greatness, its uniqueness, and its complete originality, but other words used to refer to the Universe, such as *it*, are not capitalized because that practice seems to detract from the flow of thought.

Acknowledgments

I would like to thank the inspired and dedicated publishing team who helped me shape and produce this work:

Nigel Yorwerth for his guiding hand and heart on all my books and for his unwavering efforts in promoting my work, helping me to get excellent distribution, and presenting my work to foreign publishers.

Patricia Spadaro for her enlightened editing and suggestions that helped me express the concepts in this work more clearly and accurately, allowing the I Ching wisdom to shine more brightly.

Roger Gefvert for his beautiful cover designs for all the books in my I Ching series, which reflect so well the timeless quality of the I Ching itself.

Kathy Lange and Martha Lonner for their patience and skill in layout and production, and Janet Chaikin for her expert proofing and editorial work.

 # A Brief History of the I Ching

Thousands of years ago, before the dawn of written history, legend has it that there lived a great Chinese sage known as Fu Hsi (pronounced foo shee). He is credited with leading the Chinese people from the age of hunting and fishing into the age of agriculture. As you can imagine, that was a long, long time ago—six thousand years at the earliest, and, more likely, ten thousand.

A man of enormous intellect whose psychic channels were obviously open, Fu Hsi drew forth from the Universe, over a period of time, a perfect mathematical model of itself, complete with all its conditions and stages of change—the sixty-four six-line symbols that the Chinese call the *kua* and that make up the I Ching. The complete story of how I believe Fu Hsi formulated his model can be found in my book *A Tale of the I Ching*. That book will open the heart of the I Ching to you.

To form the sixty-four kua, Fu Hsi, it is said, surveyed the vast diversities and movements under Heaven, saw the ways that the movements met and became interrelated, and saw how their courses were governed by eternal laws. He thought through the order of the outer world to its end and explored his own nature to its deepest core. He perceived the beginning of all things—things that lay unmoving in the "beyond" in the form of ideas, concepts, and forms that had yet to manifest themselves. He put himself in accord with those ideas, concepts, and forms and, in so doing, arrived at an understanding of fate.

It is also quite possible that he simply received that information in the form of a communication from the Universe as a waking dream, a sleeping dream, or a vision in meditation or that he received it in a moment of clarity while walking through the forest, as we ourselves do when we perceive a new idea. Or it could be, as one legend tells, that Fu Hsi saw a giant turtle climbing out of the Yellow River with the markings of the I Ching on its back, or, as another legend tells, that he saw a great horse with the I Ching markings on its coat. When the Universe wants to communicate with us, it uses whatever means are at hand.

Writing did not exist at the time of Fu Hsi, so his teachings were handed down in the oral tradition, with one generation faithfully teaching another for thousands of years. It was the most valuable information on the planet, and, as such, it was treasured and passed on. When writing came to China five thousand years ago, about the year

3000 BC, the I Ching readings were the first information to be recorded. During the next two thousand years, the I Ching and its teachings flourished.

In the twelfth century BC, the tyrant Chou Shin ruled. He was to be the last emperor of the Yin Dynasty. He was a cruel and heartless man who tortured people to please his equally cruel and sadistic concubine. So cruel was he that all of China lived in fear of him.

At the same time, there also lived a man named Wen, a direct descendant of Fu Hsi and a learned I Ching scholar of rare insight, who governed a small province in a remote area of western China. Wen governed his people according to I Ching principles and was therefore as much loved and respected by the people as Chou Shin was hated and feared. The people urged Wen to gather an army and overthrow the tyrant. They assured him that all the people would follow him willingly. But he replied that because he was truly a law-abiding citizen, he could not in good conscience take action against the emperor.

Unfortunately for Wen, but fortunately for the rest of us, Chou Shin heard the rumors that Wen was being asked to lead an uprising and had him arrested and put into prison. Wen was allowed to live because of his great popularity, and his time in imprisonment allowed him to make his wonderful contribution to the refinement of the I Ching.

During the year 1143 BC, the year that Wen spent in

confinement and in fear for his life, he used the I Ching's great wisdom and its divinatory powers to keep himself alive. In Wen's time, there were two versions of the I Ching, the Lien Sah and the Gai Tsen. Neither one offered any guidance other than elaborating on the six lines of each kua. During his imprisonment, Wen provided the names of the kua and described the condition or situation that each of them portrayed—what we know today as the opening paragraphs of the kua. He also changed the order of the kua established by Fu Hsi to the order currently in use in every modern version of the I Ching. (The order of the kua does not in any way affect the readings.)

In 1122 BC, Wen's oldest son, Wu, publicly denounced Chou Shin to turn public opinion against him, gathered an army, overthrew the tyrant, and became emperor. To honor his father, who had passed away, Wu posthumously bestowed upon him the title of king, and Wen was forever after known as King Wen, even though he never ruled as king.

Wu died a few years after becoming king and left his thirteen-year-old son as heir to the throne. The inexperienced youngster obviously was incapable of ruling, so Wu's brother, Tan, known as the Duke of Chou, ruled in his stead. Wen had instructed Tan in the teachings of the I Ching, and it was Tan who, during his reign as acting king, interpreted the meanings of the individual lines and added the text to each line to create the I Ching as we know it today. The I Ching was then considered complete. The year was 1109 BC, approximately thirty-one hundred years ago.

In AD 1700, the Khang Hsi editors prepared the current version of the I Ching along with commentaries from more than 380 different scholars who had written their works over a period of three thousand years. The document was completed in 1715 and is the version that everyone translates into today's version of the I Ching.

So profound was the wisdom that King Wen and his sons derived from their study of the I Ching that they were able to found a dynasty that lasted for nine hundred years, the longest in the history of China. As you might imagine, they used the I Ching to gain insight and to receive Universal guidance in making decisions.

Several hundred years later, in the fifth century BC, the great sage and scholar Confucius came on the world scene. It is said that he was a homely man, almost seven feet tall, with a hump on his back. He distinguished himself by studying court etiquette and learned it so thoroughly that the emperors sought him out for guidance. He became famous not only for his knowledge of court etiquette but also for his great common sense. At the age of fifty, Confucius began the study of the I Ching, and when he was past the age of seventy, he humorously commented, "If some years were added to my life, I would give fifty to the study of the I Ching and might then escape from falling into great errors."

Confucius wrote many commentaries regarding the I Ching. Most of these are reproduced in other volumes of the I Ching, notably the wonderful Wilhelm/Baynes translation, published by Princeton University Press (Bollingen Series XIX). Should you become so engaged with the I Ching that you wish to go beyond using it as an oracle and begin studying it, you will surely want to consult that most thorough work.

CHAPTER ONE

On the Wings of Six Dragons

The greatest deed has been accomplished—the creation of the Universe. Now that the greatest deed has been accomplished, everything else is possible.

What that means for you is that you can rise to greatness, that you can accomplish your goals, no matter how lofty, that you can be who you want and have what you want, and that everything is within your reach. Is that not wonderful?

The wisdom of the I Ching tells us:

The same intelligent, aware force that created and sustains the Universe, which IS the Universe, created and sustains us. That intelligent, creative, aware force endlessly shapes and alters us to the purpose that we will ultimately come to achieve our true nature, after which we will forever resonate with the great harmony.

The Universe brings you situations, conditions, and

events that provide you with "workout situations." Sometimes those workout situations appear as problems or events that hurt you or take something from you. In all cases, those events are there for your benefit. Have you ever had something happen to you that you thought was awful but later turned out to be a great benefit? Of course you have. That has occurred to us all. Learn to see that truth in everything that befalls you, seemingly bad events included. You will be amazed at the difference it will make in your life.

You might well ask, "How long will it take me to achieve my true nature? Ten years? Twenty? A lifetime? A hundred lifetimes? Ten thousand?"

The answer is different for each of us, but by keeping in mind the goal—to realize your true nature—and by remaining aware that the altering and shaping process through which you will achieve your goal is necessary and entirely for your benefit, you will speed joyously upward to your goal as though on the wings of six dragons.

CHAPTER TWO

How the I Ching Works

The wisdom of the I Ching has been passed along from person to person for perhaps as many as ten thousand years. In this, it is no different from any of the other old wisdom or information that has come down to us through the centuries from the people of all the ancient lands. What makes the I Ching stand apart is that there is substantiation for it in the Universe—physical substantiation.

The sixty-four kua of the I Ching were originally arranged by Fu Hsi somewhere between six and ten thousand years ago. He originally arranged them in the order shown on the next page. Two hundred years ago, Gottfried Wilhelm Leibniz, a German philosopher and mathematician, invented the binary system. It is a numerical system, using only zeros and ones, with which any number can be represented and upon which all computer language is based. Shortly after or shortly before Leibniz developed the binary system for writing numbers, someone sent him a copy of the I Ching. He inspected it and realized that if ones and zeros were substituted for the broken lines and the solid lines of

THE EARLY HEAVEN ARRANGEMENT

The chart above shows Fu Hsi's original arrangement of the kua, called the Early Heaven Arrangement. It was later revised by King Wen in 1143 BC in what came to be known as the Later Heaven Arrangement (shown on facing page), which is the arrangement that is in use worldwide today. The arrangement of the kua does not affect the readings.

THE LATER HEAVEN ARRANGEMENT

the sixty-four kua, the kua could be read as binary numbers from zero to sixty-three. In effect, Fu Hsi had developed the binary system somewhere between six and ten thousand years ago.

What is more important, in 1973 it was discovered that the sixty-four kua match perfectly the construction of the sixty-four DNA codons of the genetic code when represented in binary form. That is ample substantiation that Fu Hsi's system is based on Universal order.

Think of that. With no computers or equipment of any kind, Fu Hsi extracted from the Universe a tiny mathematical model of itself. What's even more incredible is that he applied it to the answering of questions. If you have not used the I Ching as an oracle, a source for answering questions with complete accuracy, the following brief explanation will make the process clear.

You Can Know What the Universe Knows

Because you are part of the Universe, and because time is a living entity that contains consciousness—may indeed *be* the consciousness of the Universe, permeating everything, including ourselves—you can know everything the Universe knows. All you need is a key to unlock that fount of sublime wisdom and complete information. That you have the key is unquestionable. Every time you get a new idea, you have used your key. You may like to think that you created the idea, but what you did was no less noteworthy. You channeled the idea from the Source; you used your key.

The premise of all divination is that the key exists within each of us. Divination presupposes that there is a part of us that is at one with everything, including time, and therefore knows what everything knows. The English word *divination* is derived from the Latin words meaning "deity" and also "to foretell."

For us to be able to draw from the fount of Universal wisdom, we must have a means to do so. Some people draw from the fount by praying, some by meditating, some by being quiet and focusing their attention on the subject under question or on no question at all, some by consulting with psychics or astrologers, others by interpreting dreams, and still others by manipulating coins, tarot cards, runes, yarrow stalks, or other objects.

All of the systems work, but only up to the limits of those systems and the capability of the questioner or interpreter. If, for instance, you ask a question and flip a coin to get an answer, you are limited to a yes or no answer. If you ask a question and select from a deck of cards, where each card contains several sentences of guidance printed on it, you can obtain counsel beyond yes or no. The more sophisticated the system, the more complete and detailed the answer you will receive.

If you and I decided to formulate an ideal system to

obtain answers to questions, we would want to make sure there was an answer for every question that could be asked. Fortunately, we do not have to create such a system of answers: the I Ching masterfully fills that need. It may seem difficult, even impossible, to have accomplished that task, yet one answer can be sufficient for many questions. For example, all questions regarding taking action can generally be satisfied with three answers: to take action, to take no action, or to delay taking action.

The ideal system of divination would also have to devise a method for determining how to obtain the answers that apply to specific questions. Because we are searching for cosmic answers, we must prevent ourselves from intellectually tampering with the way in which we obtain the results. We need a method that permits only the spiritual portion of ourselves—that portion that is at one with All-That-Is—to participate. The I Ching's yarrow stalk method perfectly accomplishes that end.

When you close your eyes and grasp a number of yarrow stalks from a bunch of forty-nine stalks, when you select cards whose faces you cannot see, when you choose a stone from a pile of inscribed stones whose faces you cannot see, or use similar practices, you exceed the ability of your rational mind. That is because you cannot know how many stalks were grasped, which card was chosen until its face is seen, or which stone was chosen from the pile until the inscription on its face can be read. All such methods of choosing rely completely on the intuitive ability of the questioner, on his ability to draw upon his spiritual source, which knows everything. In the words of Lao Tzu, "to feel beyond touch…to hear beyond sound…to see beyond shape, and…to tell beyond words."

Does the I Ching system of divination work? Yes. Will it work for you? Yes, as long as you seek the truth with reverence, sincerity, and good intent. It works because there is a part of you that knows the answers to all your questions and will guide you in choosing the correct answer. You are a divine being in an eternal Universe of which you are an inseparable part, and that Universe is an inexhaustible wellspring of cosmic information from which you may freely draw.

Finding the Answers to Your Questions

Fu Hsi's sixty-four kua are each made up of six lines stacked one above the other (see pages 6 and 7). The lines can be either broken (– –) or solid (—). Each kua represents a particular situation or condition, and each of the six lines of the kua has a specific explanation associated with it and represents a stage of evolution within that situation. These stages are (1) about to come into being, (2) beginning, (3) expanding, (4) approaching maximum potential, (5) peaking, and (6) passing its peak and turning toward its opposite condition.

Since every ending contains a new beginning, the ending of one kua is the beginning of another.

Fu Hsi's method for selecting the appropriate kua is unique: the manipulation of fifty yarrow stalks, one being laid aside as an observer stalk and the rest being divided and redivided eighteen times. When you ask a question using the I Ching, the answer you receive, which is in the form of a kua, tells you the situation or condition that surrounds your question and what actions you need to take or avoid to achieve a successful outcome or to bypass danger.

In your I Ching readings, you may receive one or more lines that are called moving lines. Manipulation of the yarrow stalks results in numerical answers, either sixes, sevens, eights, or nines. The lines that are obtained with sixes or nines are called moving lines and are the ones that provide information you should follow (the moving lines and how to use the yarrow stalk method with the I Ching is fully explained in my book *The I Ching: The Book of Answers*). The moving lines offer specific guidance about what action to take or not to take to bring about the result that is best for you or they give essential information relating to your question. The moving line or lines also result in the formation of a new kua, which will provide additional information relevant to your situation.

A moving line is so called because it is charged with so much energy that it turns into its opposite: a broken line turns into a solid line, and a solid line turns into a broken line. This results in a new configuration of the six lines. Only the moving lines, those obtained with sixes or nines, change into their opposite.

Here is an example of how it works. Say that in consulting the I Ching you receive kua 59, Huan (Dissolve, Disintegrate, Dissipate, Unify), which looks like ☴☵, and that your reading indicates that line 5 is a moving line. Line 5 is the fifth line from the bottom and it is an unbroken line. Because it is a moving line, it changes into a broken line, bringing about the formation of the second kua, which you will take into account in your reading. In this example, the new kua is kua 4, Mêng (Inexperience), which looks like ☶☵. The new kua describes what the situation you are asking about will become or it supplies additional information that will guide you.

What is magical about the I Ching is not its presentation of the sixty-four kua but that it provides the key to identifying which kua will correctly answer your question through the manipulation of the yarrow stalks. The ancient text specifically calls for the use of yarrow stalks (stalks from the milfoil plant) in divination. If you cannot get them from a local bookstore, you can obtain them by contacting the publisher of this book (see contact information listed at the front of the book).

With the use of yarrow stalks, you can obtain answers

to all your most important questions—accurate answers, answers that are for your highest and best good. In fact, I have recently revised my version of the I Ching and have changed its subtitle from the traditional *The Book of Changes* to *The Book of Answers*.

The I Ching says that teaching is a holy task, to be withheld from no one. Fu Hsi perceived the laws of the Universe and set them forth in the I Ching as teaching so that we could be guided, so that we could be free, so that we would no longer be subject to the tyranny of events, and so that each of us could be in charge of our own fate.

Fu Hsi spoke of the paths of life, calling the path that leads to good fortune "the way of the superior person" and the path that leads to misfortune "the way of the inferior person." The path of the superior person is what I have called here "the I Ching life." That path is narrow in one sense and broad in another. It is narrow in that it does not stray into areas of dishonesty, selfishness, debauchery, harmful intentions, and unclean living. It is broad in the sense that it encompasses everything else that is in keeping with virtue, honor, clean living, good intentions, and integrity. The chapters that follow explore how to live the I Ching life—the path to your authentic self that is filled with love, happiness, abundance, and success.

CHAPTER THREE

The Joyful Journey

Every spider web that has ever been woven is different from every other spider web. The face of every person is different from every other face. No leaf that has ever existed has been the same as any other leaf. Everything is different from everything else—*the diversification is total*. Can you not, therefore, imagine that the path to enlightenment is different for every person, must be different? The path that one person follows is not the correct path for any other person. You must follow your own path. That is the way.

You are on your path to enlightenment. You cannot be off your path. The progress you make along your path will be quick or slow according to your level of awareness. By consciously seeking enlightenment, you will progress quickly, receiving the rewards of ever-greater enjoyment, peace, success, good fortune, and well-being. You will find that moving toward enlightenment is a joyful journey.

Enlightenment is knowing the truth of your existence. It is knowing who you are in the Universal scheme and knowing how to live harmoniously within that scheme. To seek enlightenment, hold the goal of achieving enlightenment lightly in your mind. All else will occur as a result of natural law.

SEEKING ENLIGHTENMENT

You might well ask, "How do I hold enlightenment in my mind as a goal?" By your desire—your desire to know what your role is in the Universe, your desire to advance along your spiritual path, your desire to live the life of a superior person, your desire to know how others have progressed along the path toward enlightenment. By following those desires, you will, as a result of Universal law, move toward enlightenment.

Your path, like everyone's, extends to eternity. Be relaxed and cheerful; you are in the perfect hands of the Universe. You're safe. You cannot be hurt, in the Universal sense of the word.

An old story tells of a follower of the I Ching way who when confronted by a warrior threatening to cut off his head appeared unafraid, even calm. The warrior asked the man if he was not afraid of him. The man replied, "I am not afraid of death. Why should I be afraid of you?" The warrior threw down his sword and became the man's student.

The path to enlightenment is the path of the superior person. At any moment, including this one, you may decide to seek enlightenment as your goal, thereby radically altering your circumstances and making it possible for you to enjoy the great rewards that are available to everyone, withheld from no one. That you are reading this book is an indication that you have already deliberately chosen to seek enlightenment.

PROTECTING YOURSELF FROM DANGER

You can discover valuable information about your own path to enlightenment and receive specific guidance about ways to traverse that path by using the I Ching. You can also protect yourself from danger. That is one of the more important uses of the I Ching.

Many times in your life, you will be threatened by danger. For instance, suppose you were planning to travel to a part of the world that is politically unstable. If you were to use the I Ching to make the inquiry "What can I expect from traveling to that destination?" and you received kua 29, K'an (Danger), you would know that your trip would expose you to danger.

Suppose you were going to invest in the stock market and you received a reading of danger. It would be a wise course of action not to invest in the stock market at that time. You could consult the I Ching again at a later date to ask the same question.

A young man who wanted to purchase a motorcycle once asked me for advice. I suggested that he make an

I Ching inquiry. He made the inquiry, asking, "What can I expect from buying a motorcycle at this time?" The answer was kua 51, Chên (Shock). The moving line he received in his reading said, "To begin brings danger, to continue brings shock." He wisely did not buy the motorcycle at that time. A year later, he asked again and received a more favorable reading and so went ahead with his purchase.

A man in California owned a large parcel of real estate that he had to sell because the monthly payments were too much for him and he needed the money for other purposes. He put the property on the market through a broker. An agency of the State of California made an excellent offer to purchase his property.

Instead of accepting the offer, the owner made a counter-offer in which he stated he was not going to sell all of the property as he originally intended but was going to keep a portion of the property for himself. He sent the altered agreement back to the state. Then he made an I Ching inquiry to see if what he had done was the right thing. The answer was kua 5, Hsü (Waiting in the Face of Danger). The moving line, 3, said that he had made a poor start and was only attracting danger. The danger he was attracting was his inability to make the monthly payments if the state did not purchase his property.

The state wrote back to him and said they were not interested in purchasing only a portion of his property. He quickly amended his offer, agreeing to sell all of the property to them. The state wrote back and said that it had purchased another property and was no longer interested in his property. It would have been smarter for the man to have made his inquiry *before* replying to the state the first time. He could have asked, "What can I expect if I amend the offer to keep a portion of the property for myself?"

The I Ching tells us:

> *Danger has an important*
> *and beneficial use.*

Being aware of danger, you can take the necessary precautions to protect yourself from harm when danger arises. By doing this, you have used danger to further the achievement of your success and to protect what you already have.

Be Guided by What Is Within

On your path to enlightenment, it is advisable to look to others you admire for guidance. Although the path they have followed is their path, not yours, they may have useful information you can use for your own benefit. When you seek advice from others, it is always wise to listen carefully to what they have to say, but in the end make whatever decision you feel is in your best interests.

No one else can walk your path for you. No one else can achieve enlightenment for you. All anyone can do is to point you in the right direction and allow you to do the rest. The I Ching advises:

Do not allow yourself to be
led astray by a leader.

This is not to say that you should ignore a leader or good counsel from a qualified person, but it is wise to question whether a leader's course is best or honorable *for you* and then to make your own decision. Let yourself be guided by what is within you, that which is at one with everything and therefore always knows the correct action and the correct time to take that action.

TURNING BACK

Consulting the I Ching to discover answers to questions concerning taking the right action at the right time is one of the best uses of the I Ching. As you move along your path, it is a good idea to occasionally check to see whether your timing is right and your actions are in accord with your highest and best good.

It is not unusual to digress at times from your intended path. Having turned onto the path of the inferior person, it is only natural that you will feel remorse, powerful remorse, but that is a good sign. However, you must not carry remorse too far; after making whatever amends you can, continue on, having resolved to be more cautious. The

I Ching teaches:

> *In following the path of the superior person,*
> *slight digressions from the good cannot be avoided,*
> *but you must turn back before going too far.*

To follow the path of the superior person takes great courage, firm determination, and fierce perseverance. You must watch like a hungry hawk for transgressions, and if you find them, you must turn back. This is an act of self-mastery and is highly commendable. Having turned back, you will progress like a hurricane, sweeping all obstacles from your path, and supreme good fortune and great success will quickly follow.

CHAPTER FOUR

In Harmony with the Universe

To awake in the morning and take a moment to refresh yourself with the knowledge that you are a divine being in a sparkling Universe, to communicate with that sparkling Universe as though it were a dear friend, that is the start of an I Ching day. "Good morning," says the aware being, addressing All-That-Is, adding, if appropriate, "Thank you for that most wonderful sleep."

At the heart of living life according to the wisdom of the I Ching is the knowledge that the Universe is alive and aware—aware of itself and aware of you. It may seem strange at first to communicate aloud or silently with All-That-Is, with the Universe itself, but as you become more and more aware that you are being heard, that there is communication going on in both directions, you will come to cherish the gift.

Keep aware as you read this book that you are a living part, an inseparable part, of an alive, aware organism. When great grief, misfortune, or illness befalls us and no human can help, we instinctively turn to the divine for help. That is only natural, since each of us inherently knows the truth of his existence and origin. The I Ching teaches:

> *The superior person is reverent,*
> *at all times acknowledging the great Creator*
> *and the wondrousness of the Universe.*

When we see a great painting, we acknowledge the painter. When we see a great structure, we acknowledge the builder. When we see the Universe, the tiny portion of it that is visible to us, how can we fail to acknowledge its Creator? Personally, I believe that the Universe and the Creator are one. I capitalize *Universe* for the same reason that I capitalize *God*. For me, they are one and the same.

None of us can fathom how this Universe of ours began, nor can any of us foretell when or if it will end. Not one of us can even say why it or we exist. Since we can only wonder at it all, does it not seem immensely egotistical and foolish not to be reverent in the face of that awesomeness?

CHAOS AND CHANCE DO NOT EXIST

The major difference between humans and other life forms on our planet is our ability to reason and to question. For just a moment, try to deliberately free your mind from what you have been told about religion, evolution, birth, death,

God, and any other concepts you have about why you're here on earth. Think clearly, on your own, about what you know of life and the world around you.

Now, imagine if you had to tell someone what you believed about the Universe, who you are, and why you're here—just from your own personal observations and not repeating anything that anyone else has told you about God or religion. What would you tell that person? What do you make of it all? Do you take your existence for granted, without considering that you have awareness? Do you wonder what is the reason for your existence?

A friend of mine, a physicist who lives in Los Angeles, California, believes that there is no reason for our presence here on earth. He says, "We are just here." When I questioned him about his belief, he said, "There has been enough time for us to evolve into who and what we are without the intervention of any supreme intelligence. There is no discernible cause beyond natural evolution, nor does there appear to be any reason for our existence, nor does there need to be. Since I have not been able to perceive any divine being or see any evidence that a divine being exists, or has ever existed, and since I only believe in what I can prove or at least see evidence of, I choose to believe that our existence is simply a matter of evolution and our awareness is simply a product of a complex biological organism."

Is that what you believe? That we, who are this wonderful

life form—who can feel joy, love, compassion, happiness, sadness, fear, and wonder, who can create music and write poetry, who can appreciate beauty—are a product of an unthinking, unknowing, unaware, dead Universe? Are we to believe that the Universe of which we are a part, which has produced us, and from whose substance we are made is dead, while we are alive?

Are we so egotistical as to believe that we alone have awareness and intelligence and the rest of the Universe does not? Or are we to believe that we *are* the Universe, a portion of it, and that because we have intelligence and awareness, it necessarily follows that the rest of the Universe also has intelligence and awareness?

To believe that we are simply a result, one of many, of a mindless universe where chaos reigns and that we are but a chance manifestation is too lackluster for me, too empty. There is no wonder or magic in it. Neither is there any dignity or grandeur in that concept. To believe in a mindless, chaotic universe is to also believe that the future is completely uncertain, that the Universe could end at any moment, that our existence is in the hands of blind chance.

If chaos were the pervading condition and chance ruled, the Universe would not have continued for all these billions of years. If the continuation or discontinuation of the Universe were a chance occurrence, a moment-by-moment flip of the coin, and if heads meant to continue and tails meant to discontinue, in the approximate eighteen billion years since our Universe began, tails would have certainly come up at least once, ending it all. The fact that the Universe persists rules out absolutely, for me, the possibility that chaos reigns or even exists or that chance is the underlying condition of all existence. Chance and chaos only seem to exist if we do not have enough of an overview to be able to perceive the perfect order within which everything exists.

SEPARATION IS AN ILLUSION

Do you believe in God or in a Supreme Being you call by another name? If so, do you believe that God or your Supreme Being is separate from you? Many of us have been taught that, and therefore when we say the word *God*, we conjure up an image of something outside of ourselves, something from which we are, in effect, disconnected, separated.

All religions believe that a Deity, a God, a Supreme Being, by whatever name they choose to call "It," existed at the beginning of creation. They believe that everything that was created was created by and out of the substance of that Supreme Being. For instance, most versions of the Bible in the Christian religion state that in the beginning there was only God. The Bible then goes on to say that God created the earth and the heavens. Since all there was in the beginning, according to the Bible, was God, it necessarily follows that everything that God created was created from God. If the Bible is correct, it also follows that everything in the Universe is alive and aware, saturated with the power, intelligence, and awareness of that Great Being from whom it was formed.

You may not be able to perceive life in a stone, but that does not mean that a stone does not live, does not have awareness. Crystals grow and rocks crumble into dust to be taken up and used by vegetables, which are, in turn, eaten by animals, including ourselves. When we and the other animals and the vegetables die, our bodies disintegrate and are taken up to be used by yet other life forms, all alive, all aware, in an endless cycle.

If you were to peer into the heart of a stone at the atomic level, you would not see a dead, inert mass of material but a furiously whirling mini-cosmos. This mini-cosmos would look much like what you see when you look into the night sky, but its bits and pieces would be whirling at speeds near that of light.

There was a time when scientists were searching for the basic building blocks of the Universe. First they thought the smallest building blocks were molecules, then atoms. Then, when they were able to peer into the heart of the atom, they discovered even smaller bits and pieces: a nucleus, neutrons, protons, electrons, and then even smaller quarks, gluons, and neutrinos.

The smallest particles have not yet been seen, for they are too tiny and travel at furious speeds. We know of their existence only because of their footprints, the tracks they leave behind in their speeding whirl. It is their very speed that renders matter "hard." Just as a spinning airplane propeller appears to be an almost solid disk, so the whirling of the tiny particles creates the illusion of the hardness of matter.

Relatively speaking, the same distance exists between the particles in an atom as exists between the stars. To visualize the size of an atom inside an orange, for instance, imagine an orange as big as the Earth, almost 8,000 miles in diameter and with a circumference of 24,902 miles. Next, imagine golf balls whirling around inside the Earth-sized orange. That is how atoms inside an orange would look if the orange were blown up to the size of the Earth. To be able to appreciate the size of the nucleus inside the atom, take the golf-ball-sized atom inside the orange and blow it up to the size of a stadium one half mile across. Now put a grain of salt on the floor. That's the relative size of the nucleus (the grain of salt) to an atom (the stadium)—and the nucleus itself is huge in comparison to the smaller particles.

Scientists have now discovered that the smallest of the particles appear and disappear, forming from and dissolving back into seemingly empty space. However, space is not actually empty, nor is it really even space; it only appears as space because we can't see the energy that makes up space, that *is* space. It is this invisible field of energy from which matter is formed. Scientists believe there is more energy in one square half inch of space than there is in all the physical matter of the known Universe. Remember what happens when we split a hydrogen atom? There's enough energy released to destroy an entire city the size of Los Angeles.

ASK THE PERSON WHO KNOWS

Think of it—matter being created from space, an ocean of energy that intensifies, bringing "things" into being, energy changing from its primal form into another form, a physical form. The Earth, the planets, the stars, other galaxies, and ourselves are all created from the same energy. Simply stated, energy and matter are one; therefore, all is one. Because that is true, I believe that one day, when we have advanced far enough along our spiritual paths to be entrusted with the care of other parts of the Universe, we will actually be able to travel in the energy field, instantly being anywhere in the Universe.

The creation of matter from energy is the desire of the Universe to manifest itself—to manifest itself in all its myriad forms. And what are we? We, and all else that has been manifested from the energy field, are one of the ways the Universe experiences itself.

You *are* the Universe—just as much as anything in the

Universe is the Universe. *In fact, you do not have to seek immortality; you already have it. The closest you can come to a true religious experience on this planet is just being who you are at any moment.* Being who you are is a pure religious experience. If you can stay with that experience, just being a part of All-That-Is, that's enough. Instead, we go searching, chasing after masters because most of us want more than just being ourselves.

If you want more, ask the person who knows what everything knows—yourself. Use the I Ching to ask:

"Who am I in the Universal scheme of things?"

"What happens when I die?"

"Is there a life after death?"

"What is my mission on earth?"

"What do I need to know about God?"

Everything Responds to You

You might well ask, "How does this information affect me and how can I use this information to lead a better, fuller, more aware life?" Once you perceive that the Universe is alive, a living, pulsating organism that has awareness and intelligence, vast intelligence, you will come to know that the Universe and everything in it reacts to stimulation—your stimulation.

Just as you are stimulated by other people and by the manifestations of the Universe, such as weather changes and planetary and stellar influences, so the Universe is also stimulated by you. Through your mood changes, your thoughts, and your actions, through being the way you are at every moment, you continually exert an influence on everyone and everything around you.

Imagine, for example, a man who is angry all the time. Can you see how he would influence everyone around him? Can you see that in a short time he would be friendless? He would suffer from the results of his anger.

By learning the laws of the Universe that are embodied in the I Ching and by learning to live in harmony with those laws, you will become a being who forever resonates with the great harmony and you will live what the I Ching describes as "the life of the superior person." You will learn to live in a manner that brings you peaceful harmony, long-lasting good fortune, great success, and happiness. You will learn to flow with the ever-changing events around you, smoothly integrating your actions into the Universal scheme. Anger, frustration, and despair will disappear, and feelings of well-being and exhilaration will pervade you as you experience sublime success.

Sublime success is more than what most of us think of as "success"; it is the epitome of success and brings with it happiness, peace, and spiritual wholeness. Financial success without happiness, peace, and spiritual wholeness is worthless. It is better to be financially unsuccessful and happy than to be financially successful and miserable. Living life according to I Ching precepts permits you to avoid the pitfalls that beset the path of those who never give a thought to the consequences of their thoughts, words, or actions.

In *all* circumstances, what you believe determines your actions. Your actions determine your future. The choice of how you live and what becomes of you is in your own hands.

CHAPTER FIVE

The God Game

When I was a brash youngster, I sat one evening in front of my fire wondering what it would be like to be God, the popular conception of God: all powerful, all-seeing, and all-knowing. My first thought was "How boring. There's nobody to talk to, at least not on God's level, and what's there to talk about anyway when everything is known, past, present, and future? There's nothing to do that God hasn't already done, nothing to see that God hasn't already seen, and nothing to know that God doesn't already know."

The situation I imagined was intolerable, at least to my tiny, human imagination. I wondered what God would do in such a circumstance. The answer came, fully formed, as if I had swallowed a capsule with the information inside. I knew beyond any doubt, at least in my own mind, what God would do, had done. God would create a game to play.

I began to think about what the game would have to be like for me, as God, to be able to play. There were two major problems. The first was my omniscience, my all-knowing-ness. If I didn't get rid of my ability to see into the future, knowing everything, the game wouldn't be any fun. There would be no suspense, no waiting to see what was coming, no sense of mystery, and it would therefore be absolutely boring! As God, I would have already looked into the future and seen what was coming, so I would have to figure out a way around that most difficult problem. The second problem was that I needed a game board on which to play.

I solved both of those problems with one stroke: I created the Universe. Instead of playing *on* the board, I would play *in* the board. Actually, I would *be* the board. The board was made from myself, and I used up *all* of myself in creating it. (The word *universe* is derived from the Latin *unus,* meaning "one," and *versus*, meaning "to turn into." Don't you find it interesting that the creators of the word *universe* imagined One being turned into the Universe?) To create the new me, the Universe, I spread my energy out into infinity, willing it to create. To create what? Well, look around. That's what I created: All-That-Is.

The problem of my omniscience was also solved when I turned myself into all those infinitesimal bits and pieces of the Universe, because my God-awareness, God-knowledge, God-power, and God-creativity were now spread out over the totality, each little particle receiving its share. My all-knowingness and all-seeingness, which before had been concentrated and therefore potent, was now spread out over the entirety and was so reduced in potency that I could only get glimpses of the future and the past.

In the creation of the Universe, I had used up all of me. There was no little box somewhere with leftover mountain ranges, skies, galaxies, stars, or planets in it. Everything was used up and *everything was in its right place. It still is*. You cannot be out of place in the Universe. Wherever you are, that's where you're supposed to be, doing whatever it is that you're doing. Whether what you are doing will bring you good fortune or ill fortune, happiness or unhappiness depends on what you are doing and your intention in doing it, whether you intend good or evil.

THE RULES OF THE GAME

Of course, I couldn't abandon my powers without a set of rules by which the game was to be played. That would leave everything in the hands of blind chance, what people today call chaos. If I had done that and something went wrong, there would just be oblivion, as when the lights go out; and because I was/am eternal, as is my Universe, the lights would be out forever.

Because I did not want the lights to go out forever, I brought into being the laws of the Universe, the rules that would govern the game. As you might imagine, the first law I created was the law of conservation of energy, which provides that none of the energy in my newly created Universe could ever be lost or damaged, only changed.

That's because everything that exists is made from me, *is* me, and I didn't want to lose any of me.

Because I wanted to keep the game interesting, the next law I created was the law of change. That law decreed that everything in the entire Universe will be in a state of constant change and constant motion, except for the Universal laws, which will remain fixed, at least till the game is won. Please take note that I did not say won or lost. The possibility of losing is zero—there is only winning. It may take a long time to win, perhaps billions or trillions of years, but the game will be won in the end. You didn't think I would create a game that I would not win in the end, did you?

On the path to winning, it may sometimes seem as if one or more of us are losing. That's just because we are not paying attention to the rules of the game, and we've either forgotten Who-We-Are or we haven't taken the time to find out. Paying attention to the laws and working in harmony with them brings great pleasure, supreme happiness, great abundance, and the sure knowledge that everything is just the way it's supposed to be. Not paying attention to the laws brings us pain and unhappiness. Why? Because that's how we realize we're doing something that is off the path to winning. Those unpleasant experiences are showing us we have strayed from the path.

MASTERING THE GAME

The next law was that of cause and effect. That law provided that every change or action would produce a response that would be in perfect accord with the change or action. Cause and effect is a flowing of events—smooth, unbroken, and flawless, one change or action producing another—in perfect harmony, in perfect accord with the laws of the Universe. Once we learn to master the game, we will know which causes produce which effects—in other words, which actions we need to take to produce the conditions we desire.

In every situation or condition, by taking appropriate actions, we can bring about any other condition or situation of life we choose. You can see that principle clearly mirrored in the I Ching, where any kua can be changed into any other kua by changing the lines. What that means is that by taking the appropriate action in any situation, which we can derive by using the I Ching, we can change that situation or condition to any other situation or condition—illness to health, anger to joy, lack to abundance.

Because of the law of cause and effect, a rock thrown into a pond makes ripples every time. The bigger the rock, the bigger the ripples. Just as we can depend on that to be true and never be disappointed, we can depend on all the causes to produce their corresponding effects every time.

Knowing that All-That-Is responds to us as we are at every moment, we can make changes within ourselves that will produce the outer conditions that are nearest and dearest to our hearts. Would I, as God, have created it in any other way? Thus, with the law of cause and effect in action, living life in accord with my new laws would produce a wondrously happy person.

As God, I made many physical laws as well, laws that govern matter, such as the law of gravity, a force of attraction that holds celestial bodies in their orbits and that on Earth assures that things fall down and not up. As God, I created light, one of the greatest wonders of my new Universe, and a law that governs the speed of light—186,282 miles per second, which is about 670,600,000 miles per hour.

In case you do not have an idea as to the size of the Universe I created, to travel at the speed of light from where Earth is (near the outside of the Milky Way galaxy) to the center of the Milky Way galaxy takes 26,000 years. What's more, our galaxy is just one of billions. Scientists recently discovered a galaxy that is thirteen billion light-years away. That means that the light they detected from that galaxy took thirteen billion light-years to reach Earth, traveling at 186,000 miles *a second!* And that's not the farthest galaxy from Earth, just the farthest galaxy we have been able to see. The fact that the light from that distant galaxy took thirteen billion years to reach us means that that galaxy may no longer even exist.

I also created the law of evolution. That law provides that organisms will develop in ways that lead to ever-greater complexity and consciousness. Eventually, after billions of years, that law brought forth thinking beings, each one gifted with a tiny portion of all my original God powers: the power to imagine, to do, to create, and to destroy. I do not mean destroy in the total sense of the word (I left that power out when I created the law of conservation of energy). No part of All-That-Is can really be destroyed. What appears to be destroyed is actually transformed and returned to its original energy state, as when paper burns and turns into heat. The total amount of energy is still there; it's just in a different form.

TIPPING THE SCALES TOWARD WINNING

Because I had spread myself out over the entirety of the Universe in vast amounts of infinitesimal bits and pieces, I had lost my total omniscience. Since I wanted us to know when we were on the path to winning or losing the game, I created all the variations of pain and joy. Whenever we felt happiness, ecstasy, exhilaration, peace, pleasure, love, wonder, reverence, thankfulness, joy, or feelings like these, we would be on the path to winning. Whenever we felt unhappiness, frustration, hopelessness, avarice, hatred, greed, thoughtlessness, anger, revengefulness, ingratitude, pain, or feelings like these, we would be on the path toward losing.

Once we learned to recognize the signs of winning and losing, we could make the necessary adjustments to our thoughts and actions so we would remain on the path to winning. As God, I made the path to winning more pleasurable so we would be encouraged to follow it.

Because I had created eternity within which to play, I rigged the game by tipping the scales toward winning, because never to win through all eternity would be the same as losing, and I didn't want to lose. To tip the scales toward winning means that my Universe is favorably inclined. It means that there is slightly more light force than dark, that the more favorable outcome is favored over the less favorable outcome, and that we have a better chance of achieving our goals than not. It means that everything has a better chance of working out in our favor than not.

Would I, knowing I was creating a game for myself to play, create it any other way? Would you?

At some point in time, we will all win. In my Universe, we cannot lose. We are indestructible children of a golden Universe. We *are* the Universe, a part of it. *We are Me.* Remember that and you will play the game differently, with more confidence, more love, more enthusiasm, and more playfulness, with more of a carefree attitude, with more trust, and with more care for your fellow humans. And why not? Real separation is an illusion in my Universe. All, truly, is one.

THE OBJECT OF THE GAME

So that I would be able to enjoy what I had done to the fullest, I created the law of free will. That law provides that all thinking beings can do exactly as they please without reservation. It is *total* free will, unbounded and without limitation. As God, I wanted to be able to play the game and do exactly as I pleased. I wanted to be able to experience anything and everything, which is why I created the game in the first place. Therefore, you, as God, may do exactly as you please. The more inventive you are and the more you push beyond the boundaries of your experience, the better—but remember, the unbreakable, unbending law of cause and effect is also part of the game. You *will* reap what you sow; therefore, be careful in what you do.

When any one of us finally perceives who he or she is, it is like opening the greatest gift of all time and finding out that you get to keep it *forever!* The moment you come to know Who-You-Are, you will also know what I have done (what you have done) and I will be able to experience that through you. What a thrill!

The game, of course, had to have an object. So, what is the object of the game? For all thinking beings to become aware of Who-They-Are.

Using our free will, our intellect, our intuition, and our perception, we will finally figure out Who-We-Are. Every single thinking being does not have to figure it out on his or her own. When *most* of us have figured out Who-We-Are, a point of critical mass will be achieved, at which time everyone will become aware of Who-They-Are and the game will be won. That will be a time of exultation and ecstasy and will create a climax of joy so intense that it will eclipse even the moment I created the Universe. Instantly, all parts of me will come back together again in the sheer joy of unity, knowing we are all one. I will be totally pleased with me.

So, once I had spread out my entire Being to infinity and to eternity, willing it to create, and once I had a board in which to play and rules that governed the game—rules that even I couldn't break—the game was on and I could play. Welcome to the game!

CHAPTER SIX

Cause and Effect

In our Universe, the law of cause and effect is absolute. The law of cause and effect in physics, which deals with the world of matter and energy, says, "For every action, there is an equal and opposite reaction." In metaphysics, the law of cause and effect is different. It says, "For every action there is a response, and the response is in perfect accord with the action." *Meta* means "more than" or "beyond," and *physics* refers to the physical world, so metaphysics describes the world beyond the physical. In the metaphysical application of the law of cause and effect, living the life of a superior person will always bring you great good fortune and happiness.

One of the most powerful effects in your life is brought about by Who-You-Think-You-Are. The moment your brain became functional, you began to build an image of who and what you believe yourself to be. All the events of your life have helped to create that image, the self-image of Who-You-Think-You-Are. Whenever you speak, act, and think,

Who-You-Think-You-Are determines what your words, actions, and thoughts will be.

WHO-YOU-THINK-YOU-ARE

You continually project Who-You-Think-You-Are. Whenever you meet someone or walk into a room or consider taking on a new project, it is Who-You-Think-You-Are who walks into the room, who introduces himself, and who considers the new project. Who-You-Think-You-Are determines how you stand, whether you hold yourself proudly erect or whether you slouch.

If you know or believe yourself to be untruthful, cowardly, unfair, clumsy, a poor public speaker, or weak-willed or to have any number of other poor characteristics, that's the image you will hold in your mind and the image you will project. That image forms the basis for all the decisions you make in life. Similarly, if you know yourself to be honorable, strong, brave, fair-minded, generous, clear-headed, or articulate or to have any number of other good characteristics, that is the image you will project, and that image forms the basis for the decisions you make. According to the law of cause and effect, the ideas you have about who you are will produce commensurate results, bringing into your life either happiness or unhappiness, good fortune or misfortune.

Who-You-Think-You-Are changes as you change. By taking on the characteristics of the superior person, characteristics that are clearly defined within this book, you will come to see yourself in a new light. Old images of Who-You-Think-You-Are that have existed in your mind, images that may be holding you in place and preventing you from getting ahead, will fall away to be replaced by new images that will speed you successfully toward your goals. New characteristics will develop within you that will bring you good fortune and sublime success. Remember, according to the law of cause and effect, the rest of the Universe is *required* to respond to you as you are at every moment.

CHARACTER AND A LIFE OF HAPPINESS

The I Ching has much to say about developing good character in order to create a life of happiness. "If you are not as you should be," says this ancient book of wisdom, "can anything happen except that you fall into a pit of your own creation?" Elsewhere in the great book it is stated, "Even the best opportunity in the hands of the wrong person comes to nothing." To help develop good character by living in harmony with the ways of the Universe, you can use the I Ching to ask questions such as:

"How can I build good character?"

"In what area do I need improvement?"

One aspect of good character that the I Ching addresses is how to conduct yourself in your pursuit of happiness. It says:

> *Mad pursuit of pleasure*
> *never takes one to the goal.*

No matter what your goal is, if you examine your motive for choosing the goal, you will discover that you have chosen it because you believe that it will bring you happiness. However, if you seek your happiness in the mad pursuit of pleasure, you will experience only temporary sensory enjoyment and you will never arrive at your goal.

Another aspect of developing good character is being authentic—being true to your real nature. Speaking about the importance of honesty and authenticity, the I Ching advises:

> *It is better to go on foot than ride*
> *in a carriage under false pretenses.*

This saying tells us that it is better to go honorably on foot and do without than to ride in a fine carriage under false pretenses and thereby lose honor. If you pretend abundance when in fact you are in need, those who would aid you will not because they will either believe you to be abundant or recognize your pretense and consider you to be unworthy. Furthermore, by pretending you have something when you do not, you diminish yourself in your own eyes and lose self-respect. Self-respect, therefore, is a product of Who-You-Think-You-Are.

The law of cause and effect and the development of good character also comes into play in how you treat others. The I Ching says:

> *Pleasant manners succeed*
> *even with irritable people.*

If you do not allow the irritability of others to affect your own pleasant conduct, your pleasant conduct will then influence them. By treating others well, you cause others to treat you well in turn. Because of your thoughtfulness and courtesy, you will gain the respect of others. Learn to see yourself as a pleasant person, courteous and respectful, and learn to do those things that a courteous and respectful person would do.

Avoiding Arrogance

When Amy was in her junior year in high school, she discovered how powerful good character can be. Amy was intelligent and attractive. She received excellent grades, actually the highest grades in all her classes, and even won the junior achievement award for being the best student in her sophomore and junior classes. Amy was also an equestrian and won many gold medals for horsemanship. She was high scorer on her volleyball team but was not elected captain, although she wanted that recognition.

Amy's goal was to be president of her senior class, but since she was not one of the more popular students, that goal seemed out of reach. She tried to become more popular by letting her classmates know that her parents were financially well off, that her father was the president of a large corporation, that she went to exotic places on her vacations, that she was a good rider of horses, that she won medals in competition, that she lived in a lovely home and drove a nice car. Her classmates, however, were unimpressed and did not seem to want her as a friend.

Amy knew that to achieve her goal of being senior class president she had to secure the help of several key students that the other students liked and respected. She talked to several students that she thought most of her classmates respected and liked. She reminded them that she was high scorer on the volleyball team, that she had twice won best student-of-the-year award, and that she was a champion equestrian rider. But no matter what she said, she was unable to enlist their aid in support of her goal.

She didn't know why she couldn't gain the assistance of the key players in her class since she was obviously well qualified, so she talked to her dad about it. He didn't know why either, but he suggested she do an I Ching reading. Amy had never done one before, so her dad helped her formulate the question. Using the I Ching she asked, "What do I need to do to be more popular in school and achieve my goal of becoming senior class president?"

Amy received the answer of kua 15, Ch'ien (Modesty, Humbleness, Moderation). That kua said that she could expect a modest success. It counseled her that people who boast or brag fail in winning the support of the people. Amy realized her boasting had worked against her. The kua also said that if she attempted too much, she would end by succeeding in nothing. "Perhaps," she thought, "I have set my sights too high."

The moving line in her reading was line 3, which states: "If you work hard and persevere, you will achieve your goal and earn great recognition. You face danger in that it is difficult to remain humble in the face of acclaim, but this is essential to your continued success. If you remain modest, you will obtain followers who will be happy to work with you. Confucius said, 'When a man does not boast of his efforts and achievements and count his merits a virtue, he is a man of great understanding and worth; for all his merits, he does not put on airs and is willing to be in a subordinate position. Noble of nature and reverent in his conduct, the modest man is therefore able to succeed.' Persevere until you reach your goal, and you will have good fortune and success. Remember, however, to share the credit with others."

Amy's father pointed out to her that the main counsel of line 3 was to remember not to boast, to be willing to be in a subordinate position, and to share the credit with others. Because line 3 is a moving line, it turns into its opposite, as I explained in chapter two. It turns from an unbroken to a broken line and forms a new kua, kua 2, K'un (Open, Receptive Yielding, Willing to Follow). The text of kua 2 states:

"Sublime success will come to you if you are willing to follow good advice, are open and receptive to new information, yield to others' ideas and wishes, follow wise leaders who have worthy goals, work hard, cooperate, and avoid taking on leadership. If you try to lead, you will go astray and will fail to achieve the sublime success promised in this kua. Seek out like-minded people to help you, and, if you find them, either join with them or have them join with you, but do not attempt to lead them. If you must carry on alone, do so, but seek guidance all the same.

"You will enjoy the sublime success promised by this kua only if you adhere strictly to its attributes, which are receptive, yielding, submissive, and willing to follow. Avoid arrogance. The Universe supports those who are modest and brings down those who are arrogant. If you are the leader, fulfill your duties of leadership, but not without following the advice of those who can offer you wise counsel. Seek information from every source, ask for help, and trust your advisors. This is a time when following rather than leading will benefit you most. The success promised by this kua is sublime, meaning that it is not only success in terms of abundance, but also success that is endowed with greatness of spirit and therefore benefits the whole of the people."

Amy followed the advice. She went to the most popular person in the class and offered her help in getting him elected as president. She also asked his help in getting her elected as his vice president. He asked what her qualifications were. She did not say anything other than that she was a hard worker and would support him completely with all her efforts. He agreed to partner with her, and after a high-spirited and lengthy campaign they were both elected.

DISCOVERING WHAT ACTIONS TO TAKE

You now know that because of the law of cause and effect you can produce any kind of effect you desire by the actions you take, but you may not know which actions to take to produce the results you want. By using yarrow stalks with the I Ching, you can find out. The I Ching will help you discover which actions will produce results that are consistent with your highest and best good and which actions will create pitfalls and disharmony for you and should therefore be avoided. You only need to ask the I Ching for guidance.

If you want to be wealthy, healthy, loved, or anything else, the I Ching can help you determine what actions will produce those effects in any situation you are facing. For instance, you can inquire:

"What action should I take to improve my income this year?"

"How can I improve my relationship with my friends?"

"What remedial action should I take to return to a state of health?"

"What should I do to improve myself?"

"How shall I respond to this new job offer?"

The law of cause and effect is powerful and unerring, and following the path of the superior person unerringly produces and maintains happiness—deep down, soul-drenching happiness. As you progress through this book, you will have the opportunity to learn more about the characteristics of a superior person. As you take on those qualities yourself, natural law will do the rest.

CHAPTER SEVEN

Fate

Your fate is not determined by chance but by all that has gone before in your life and the manner in which you have responded to new events. Good fortune is not "good luck" by a chance occurrence, but it is something you have earned and is the result of a long series of events that have led to that moment. Similarly, ill fortune is not "bad luck" that happens by chance but is the result of a long series of events that have led to that moment. It is a needed tap on the shoulder from the Universe, telling you that you have strayed from the path of the superior person.

It is said of the I Ching:

> *Neither far nor near,*
> *Neither dark nor deep,*
> *Is hidden from it.*

By using the I Ching, you can see into the heart of everything. This ancient system and text will help you determine what actions will be in your highest and best interests, and therefore you can use it to create your fate.

With the aid of the I Ching, you can actually bring about your own good fortune. You can ask anything of the I Ching, as long as you ask sincerely and with reverence. In so doing, you will soon come to discover that your higher consciousness, one with the Universe, is an unerring guide, a tool with which you can create your future.

After you have used your higher consciousness to gain answers, ponder the answers to discover their subtleties. By following the guidance you have received and by acting in accord with that which is highest and best within you, you will, as a result of natural law, achieve supreme success and experience only sublime good fortune. That is how you create your fate.

SHOCK CAN BRING SUCCESS

The Universe has many facets, from terrifying to playful, from destructive to nurturing. Kua 51, Chên, is "Shock, The Arousing." To receive this as an answer means the person asking the question has received or will receive a powerful shock, either physical, mental, emotional, or financial. The shock usually brings fear and trembling in its wake but is, in actuality, a gift of the Universe. When All-That-Is manifests itself in its terrifying forms, such as storms, earthquakes, fires, hurricanes, tragedies, or other severe shocks, the wise person examines his life to see whether he is living in accord with the highest principles. He takes stock of himself and orders his life. He searches for and seeks to improve any faults, resolving to be a better person. He does not ignore the tap on the shoulder sent to him by the aware, loving Universe of which he is a part.

Years ago, I was gathering rocks for my flower garden. I had climbed about five feet into a thirty-five-foot ravine and was prying loose a rock of about 150 pounds from the top edge of the ravine when my feet slipped from under me and I slid the remaining thirty feet to the bottom. The rock, which I had pried loose, was rolling down the steep slope after me. It landed on my head, creating a three-inch gash. The force of the blow drove me to the ground with such force that two bones in my hand were broken and welts were raised on my knees. I was afraid to reach up and feel my head because I thought I might feel my brain through the hole that I imagined must be there.

As I lay in the mud, amazed that I was still alive and even more amazed that I had not lost consciousness, I wondered, "What good thing will come to me as a result of this blow to my head?" As it turned out, keeping aware that the blow to my head was for my benefit was a key ingredient of the experience.

I went home and stood under a trickle of water from the shower and cleansed the wound. Later that day, I went to the doctor's office and had the wound stitched. Two weeks later, I did an I Ching reading to find out what getting hit on the head was all about. I received as an answer kua 51, Chên (Shock, The Arousing). The text read: "A manifestation of God. Shock brings success. It terrifies for a hundred miles, but the person who receives the shock does not let fall the sacrificial spoon and chalice." According to the text, I had received a shock that was a gift of God and, in the midst of experiencing the shock, I had kept my awareness that the shock was a gift and that it was for my benefit. I wondered what the benefit could be.

Several weeks later, I did an I Ching reading and discovered what the gift was. The blow to my head had opened channels in my brain that permitted clearer communication with my higher consciousness in relation to the I Ching. Passages in the I Ching that had long been obscure to me became clear. The answers to new readings were as clear as though I were talking with a wise grandfather who knew all things and had my absolute good at heart.

What a treasure for me! I would have gladly suffered the blow many times over to gain that precious gift, for with it I am now able to better create a more favorable fate for myself and to walk more harmoniously with All-That-Is. Not only that, I have written ten books on the I Ching since that time.

Whenever anything happens to you that seems un-fortunate, even if it is hurtful or takes something precious from you, see it as a beneficial occurrence. It may not be immediately apparent what the benefit is, but by treating the event *as though* it occurred for your benefit, you will preserve your good feelings. By acting in accord with those good feelings, you will, as a direct result of cause and effect, bring about a happy result.

Sometimes, if you don't discover on your own that you have strayed from the path of the superior person, it takes a shock to wake you up. Your job is to be grateful for the shock, to recognize it as the signpost that it is, and to set your feet once more upon the path of good fortune. Failing that, you will most likely incur other shocks. In the Universe, there is no such thing as "reaching the bottom." The Universe has an endless supply of shocks it can deliver.

You Live in a Beneficial Universe

The Universe in which we live is inclined in our favor, which is also to say that it is inclined in its own favor, since we and it are one. Being beneficially inclined is how and why the Universe persists. Were it not that way, everything would have self-destructed long ago. An alive and aware Universe will not destroy itself.

One of the reasons I strongly recommend the ancient use of yarrow stalks in divination rather than the modern coin method is that the three coins, being limited to heads or tails, do not have sufficient mathematical possibilities to adequately represent the continual unfolding of the

Universe. The forty-nine yarrow stalks do possess sufficient mathematical possibilities. (You can read a full discussion of the yarrow stalk method versus the coin method in my book *The I Ching: The Book of Answers*.)

After using the I Ching for only a short while, you will see clearly that your fate is in your own hands and that while you may have heretofore created your future unknowingly and with sorrowful results, you can now create it knowingly and with joyous results. The I Ching tells us:

> *The way of the superior person*
> *is to be joyous of heart,*
> *yet concerned in thought.*

The superior person is "concerned in thought" because he knows that all periods of prosperity are followed by times of decline and that all people are not as they should be. He therefore takes thought for the future and exercises caution in his dealings with people. Nonetheless, no matter how concerned he is in thought or how weighty those thoughts may be, his concerns are never enough to dim his inner joy because, above all, he remains aware that he is an indestructible child of an eternal, golden Universe.

As you travel along your path toward enlightenment, keep a joyous outlook on life. It will be of enormous benefit to you in creating your fate to understand that you are here forever—that you are truly eternal, as is the Universe of which you an inseparable part. Perhaps your life has not been very enjoyable this time around and you don't like the thought of being "eternal." That's understandable, but you must come to understand that you *are* a Universal life form, manifested on earth to perfect yourself as a divine incarnation, and perfect yourself you must. Read the opening paragraphs of chapter one again.

DETERMINING YOUR OWN FATE

In determining what your fate will be, it is well to keep in mind that as you traverse your path to enlightenment, you will encounter many obstacles. The way you see and respond to these obstacles can make all the difference in the outcome of events. To receive the most benefit from all events, even difficult ones, first realize that the obstacles are there completely for your benefit. Remember that even the worst thing that can happen to you will be of great benefit. Second, know that the obstacles are most often there as signposts telling you that you are slightly or greatly off course. Third, understand that the obstacle is a workout situation designed to strengthen certain areas within you that need strengthening.

A workout situation is a problem or difficulty you are experiencing in your life. By solving the problem, you will gain strength, awareness, and capability. After a lifetime of seeing problems as bothersome, troubling difficulties, the change to seeing them as beneficial workout situations will be a welcome one. At first this change may seem a difficult one to make, but you can do it. The rewards are colossal.

About fifteen years ago, an old friend of mine was sitting at my kitchen table having breakfast with me and he said, "I have the worst luck choosing women. The last nine women I have had relationships with have all turned out to be nasty, argumentative shrews." I replied, "The last nine women you chose were all sweet, gentle, loving creatures that you turned into nasty, argumentative shrews."

He got up from the table, said something nasty to me, and left. I did not hear from him for four years. One day I received a phone call from him from Hawaii. He was married, had a one-year-old son, and he was calling to tell me that I had been right in my assessment of what he had been doing with the women he had chosen. He said that he no longer did that and that he was wonderfully happy with his wife.

The previous nine women in his life had been workout situations, but he had not realized that at the time. If he had, he would have used his best efforts to create harmonious relationships with them *by making changes within himself,* to which they would have responded beautifully.

The I Ching teaches that success comes when you meet your fate and all obstacles with honesty and resolution:

*Only a person who goes to meet his
fate resolutely will be equipped
to deal with it adequately.*

To meet fate resolutely means that you have the determination to overcome whatever fate may bring, that you will not succumb to folly or temptation, and that you will not be turned aside from your chosen course. Only a strong or courageous person can stand up to his fate and overcome all obstacles. His fierce determination enables him to endure to the end.

With strength or courage, you can face things exactly as they are, without any sort of self-deception or illusion. When you have that attitude, a light develops out of events whereby you can recognize the path to success. By making this strong commitment, you actually cause favorable events to occur that would otherwise not have occurred. A person capable of that kind of commitment can reach any goal.

Keep aware of who and what you are as you become involved in the affairs of the world. Don't forget that you are an indestructible child of a golden Universe. The greatest deed, the creation of the Universe, has already been accomplished. In the face of that, all else is possible.

CHAPTER EIGHT

Relationships

A relationship is like a garden. To create a condition that will cause your plants to thrive and produce abundantly, you must weed, water, fertilize, communicate with, and care for the plants in your garden. You must also know about the special needs of the plants you're caring for. Some need more or less light than others, some need more or less water than others, and some need special fertilizers.

To create a wonderful, long-lasting, fruitful relationship, you must create a favorable condition within which your relationship will thrive and endure, and to do this you must know about the special needs of your partner. Most importantly, to have your relationship last, you must cultivate the quality of endurance within yourself.

To enjoy a meaningful way of life, and to produce long-lasting effects, the ability to endure must be firmly established within you.

To endure is to continue to the end—to continue in the face of obstacles, pain, fatigue, frustration, opposition, or hardship. Endurance is a state that is not worn down by anything. To achieve the goal of endurance so that your relationships will survive through the difficulties, failures, successes, and changes that all relationships encounter as part of the human condition, it is necessary to fix your mind on the goal of endurance. Once you have committed yourself to that goal, you will make all decisions that affect your relationship with that goal in mind, and as a process of natural law—cause and effect—your relationships will endure.

Suppose you are in a love relationship and your mate has not learned or been taught to feel secure about relationships. Suppose there is a person with whom you are friendly and whose company you enjoy, but your friendship with that person causes your mate to feel insecure and jealous. What do you do?

If you are committed to an enduring and healthy relationship, you'll explain the situation to your friend who is the object of your mate's jealousy and, at least for a while, you'll put your relationship with that person on hold. Once you have created a safe atmosphere within which your love relationship can thrive and you have built a secure base for your partner, you can enjoy relationships with others without having that insecure feeling of jealousy arise in your partner.

You may think to yourself, "If I have to stop seeing my

friend because my mate is insecure, is the relationship worth it? Why does everything I do have to be to done in the light of my decision to protect and preserve the relationship?" The answer is that for relationships to endure, that kind of thoughtfulness and care is required. Wouldn't you like to have someone care about you in that way?

In essence, the decisions you make when you don't have a mate are oftentimes different than the decisions you need to make when you become a partner in a relationship. It is not enough to say that you will treat your partner in the same fashion you would like to be treated. Your partner may require care beyond what you need. Everyone's needs are different, so in nurturing a relationship it is important for you to find out what the needs of your mate are and to provide for them.

COMMUNICATION AND THE REAL YOU

Communication is probably the single most important aspect of creating an enduring relationship. To be able to communicate freely and productively, you must create a condition where the communication can freely take place, a safe atmosphere for you and your partner. Within that safe atmosphere, each of you can openly speak to the other without fear of incurring anger, criticism, or reprisal.

If your partner tells you something in confidence, for example, and a week later you use it against your partner, chances are you will have destroyed the safe atmosphere and communication will become difficult, if not impossible. Similarly, if your partner tells you something personal and you become angry, you have most likely destroyed the safe atmosphere wherein those types of confidences can be exchanged. Set some ground rules with your partner that will ensure that each of you can freely and openly communicate thoughts and feelings to the other without fear of reprisal.

One of the main requirements for being able to communicate freely and productively is that both partners know who is "the real you." By that I mean that both partners need to understand themselves and each other in the light of their past experiences. To achieve such understanding, both partners must communicate to each other all the important experiences they have shared with all the other important people in their lives, including parents or surrogate parents, close friends, and other partners in love relationships.

Relationships from the past have created impressions and behavior patterns that carry over into the current relationship, affecting it in many ways. Because each partner has had different experiences, each will react differently to the ever-unfolding events of the relationship. To be able to understand why a partner reacts to an event the way that he or she does is critical to being able to cope with the reaction. Here is an example.

Cory and Tiffany lived together for three years. Every

Christmas, Thanksgiving, or vacation time, there was great dissension. Tiffany started fights on those occasions for no obvious reason, destroying the harmony of the holiday. Cory walked on eggshells to avoid dissension at holiday times, but no amount of caution could save the day from disaster. Tiffany was by far the stronger of the two personalities. She was an aggressive, outgoing sales agent for an insurance company, while Cory was a quiet, unassertive computer programmer. Cory felt helpless and didn't know how he could remedy the situation. He asked Tiffany if she would go for counseling, but the suggestion only made her angry.

One day, Cory came to me and told me of the problem. I suggested he use the I Ching to receive guidance and showed him how to do a reading. Using the I Ching, he asked, "What can I do to help Tiffany solve her problem of ruining our holidays?" The answer he received was kua 18, Ku (Correcting Deficiencies). The ancient text talks about correcting deficiencies caused by the mother or the father.

In his reading, Cory obtained the bottom line of the kua with a six, which meant that it was a moving line and therefore held meaning for Cory. The bottom line stated: "Correcting deficiencies caused by the father. You are in a weak position without much strength and will not receive any help, but the deficiency can be corrected by hard work. There is danger in the situation, so caution is required, but in the end, good fortune."

Based on the results of his reading, I suggested that Cory talk with Tiffany about the holidays she had shared with her parents. Because the kua said that Cory was in a weak position without much strength and because he told me of Tiffany's anger when he had brought up the subject, I suggested that he start the conversation by reminiscing with Tiffany about his own holiday times spent with his parents. That would create the safe atmosphere for Tiffany to talk about her own family holidays.

Bolstered by the reading, which said that hard work was required but in the end good fortune would come, one evening Cory talked with Tiffany about the times he had spent with his family at various holidays. Tiffany commented that the holiday times she had spent with her mother and stepfather were filled with dissension and anger. Tiffany's mother and father had gone through a messy divorce when Tiffany was four years old, and her mother remarried a year later. Her mother and stepfather moved several states away from her father, and Tiffany rarely saw her father after that. When Cory asked why holidays with her mother and stepfather were so upsetting, Tiffany refused to talk about it and became somewhat distant.

As I discussed in chapter two, in I Ching readings the moving lines result in the formation of a new kua that gives you more information about your situation. In Cory's case, the new kua into which 18 transformed, by virtue of the bottom moving line, was kua 26, Ta C'hu (Great Restraint). Since Cory's question was about what he could do to help Tiffany, the text of kua 26 meant that Cory should strongly restrain himself in his responses to Tiffany regarding what she would tell him about her prior family history. Cory wisely did not press the issue, but a few days later began to talk once more about the times he had spent with his parents during holidays. After a while, Tiffany again offered the comment that the time she had spent with her parents at holidays was a disaster. Cory only said, "Oh?" suggestively and the tale was finally told.

PAST CONDITIONING

Tiffany told Cory that her stepfather was a retired army man who saw himself as a tough guy, a hard taskmaster. Unfortunately, he also had a sadistic nature. Immediately after he married Tiffany's mother, he began to mentally dominate five-year-old Tiffany. His favorite ploy to get Tiffany to do what he wanted was to create the illusion that he had a wonderful surprise in store for Tiffany in the future.

He would say, for example, "Wait until you see what I bought for you for Christmas! You're going to love it!" He would make that statement four or five months before Christmas. Then the next time he wanted Tiffany to do something that she didn't want to do, he would say, "If you don't do it, I won't give you your Christmas present." He would constantly use the threat of not giving her the present right up until Christmas morning, when he would cause a nasty argument. As a result, there would be no present, no matter how good Tiffany had been. Her stepfather destroyed every Christmas day and blamed it each time on Tiffany.

Similarly, her stepfather would promise a wonderful vacation. He would talk for weeks about the vacation, all its wonders, and the fun they would have. Then, when he wanted Tiffany to obey him, he would threaten her with the loss of the vacation. "If you don't do what I tell you to do, I won't take you on the vacation I told you about." He would keep that up until the day of the vacation. Then, the morning they were to leave, he would cause an argument that would result in the loss of the vacation, always blaming the loss on Tiffany. The same scenario unfolded every Thanksgiving, Fourth of July, Halloween, Easter, and Labor Day weekend.

This torturous behavior kept up until Tiffany was about ten, when she started to rebel. She wouldn't wait for her stepfather to ruin the holiday; she would do it herself, and quickly. In this way, she protected herself from hurt and disappointment. That was the conditioning that she was bringing into her relationship with Cory.

Kua 26 also indicated that Cory would benefit by helping Tiffany in earning her living (in other words, in her job). To that effect, he designed a computer program that greatly assisted her in keeping track of her clients. The kua also stated that he would benefit from undertaking a major project. In accordance with that advice, Cory began to look into the purchase of a home for himself and Tiffany.

The last part of the kua said that Cory would benefit by studying the deeds of our ancient heroes and familiarizing himself with great sayings of antiquity, which he interpreted to mean that he would benefit by talking to someone who had great experience in the field of psychology. He went to see a psychologist and thoroughly acquainted himself with Tiffany's problem.

Step by step, as Cory took to heart and acted on the guidance he had received from the I Ching, not only did the holiday dissension disappear but other good things came to fruition. Within a year, Tiffany and he shared wonderful holidays together, they lived in a new home, and Tiffany was earning more money, thanks to Cory's computer program.

No matter how often I do readings with the I Ching, I never fail to be amazed at the accuracy of the readings and the way the answers fit the questions so perfectly. Using the I Ching as a tool to help maintain a relationship is wonderfully effective, no matter what circumstance you are facing. You can ask questions such as:

"What can I do to strengthen my relationship?"

"What can I do to help my mate?"

"What should I be paying attention to now regarding my relationship?"

"How will my relationship be affected if I take this new job that has been offered?"

WE BRING OUT THE QUALITIES IN OTHERS

Very few relationships come to us exactly as we want them, but with the proper care we can shape them into enduring pillars of strength and beauty within which great joy can be experienced and great deeds can be accomplished. We must also keep in mind that we have the ability to bring out the best and the worst in others.

A friend who was experiencing the ending of a relationship he had enjoyed for two years was lamenting that he was "a very bad chooser of women." This story is much the same as the one in chapter seven regarding the man who turned his mates into shrews. The man who was ending his two-year relationship said the women he picked seemed to be flawed in some way or another, and in the end the flaw caused the breakup of the relationship. "Why do all the women I choose for relationships have fatal flaws?" he asked.

I told him that the women he chose did not have "fatal flaws" but that it was he who was evoking, through his own behavior, what seemed to him to be fatal flaws in his mates. I explained that we all have the full range of potential within ourselves to be either great and wonderful or mean and nasty. It is we ourselves who bring out the good or bad qualities in our mates by being the way we are at every moment. In the same way, our own good and bad qualities are brought out by the people with whom we have relationships.

He took the information to heart and saved his relationship by going to his girlfriend and telling her it was he who had been at fault and asked for another chance. His complete turnaround melted her heart, and over a period of a year they created a first-class relationship.

TRUTHFULNESS AND TRUST

Another major factor in successful relationships is truthfulness. Relationships require complete integrity. The first time you lie or are untrue to your partner, you condemn yourself and your partner to a second-class relationship. First-class relationships are possible only in an atmosphere of total trust.

If you are in a relationship and have already been less than completely truthful with your partner, you can remedy this situation by making your partner aware of your untruthfulness and of your intention to be honorable in the future. That type of remedial action may at times result in the loss of the relationship, but it is better not to have the relationship at all than to exist in a condition of dishonor and distrust and share a relationship that is less than all it could be.

I know a man who had been unfaithful to his mate. When I suggested to him that he be truthful and tell her of his infidelity, he told me, "She couldn't handle the truth." The fact is, he's the one who couldn't handle the truth. He was afraid of the consequences of the truth. He was afraid that his mate would leave him if she found out he had been unfaithful to her. So they were forced to live a lie, existing in a relationship where there was no trust. As a result, their relationship went from bad to worse and ended in divorce.

The I Ching advises:

The superior person is completely sincere
in his thoughts and actions.

That means your actions should be simple and unpretentious and that you should not pretend love or other emotions that you do not feel. Like all false illusions, pretending only brings hurt and despair to everyone and bodes ill for the pretender. Besides, keeping up a pretense is tiresome and creates a poor self-image. There is no need to pretend or deceive; fix your eyes on the path of the superior person, be yourself, and all else will be accomplished as a result of natural law.

MAKE YOURSELF HAPPY

In all relationships, be sure to maintain your individuality and take responsibility for yourself and your happiness.

Do not make the mistake of relying on your mate or your friends or relatives for your happiness. The I Ching tells us:

If you depend on your relationships for
your happiness, you will either be happy or
sad as your relationships rise and fall.

To avoid such a fate, rather than depending on others for your happiness, wed your happiness to that which endures: the path of the superior person. A quiet, self-contained joy, desiring nothing from without and resting content with everything, allows you to remain independent and free— free in the quiet security of a heart fortified within itself.

Therefore, while you should take the best possible care of your relationships, remember that you came into this world alone and you shall depart from it alone. In the meantime, do not burden your relationships with the task of making you happy. Make yourself happy by the quality of your own thoughts and by what you know of the Universe and the way it works. When you have accomplished that goal, you will be able to make your partner happy because your partner will be in the company of a happy person.

CHOOSE CAREFULLY

While you must take responsibility for the fate of your relationships, you must also make careful choices to begin with. The I Ching advises:

In friendships and close relationships,
you must make a careful choice.

Certain people uplift you; others pull you down. Certain people give you strength; others sap your energy. Choose carefully. Good friends, like good neighbors, are an endless benefit, a treasure. Bad relationships and bad friends can ruin a lifetime. Following the path of the superior person permits a natural selection that will find you only with the best-quality friends. In the I Ching, we learn:

The superior person is never led into
baseness or vulgarity by community of
interests with people of low character.

Sometimes, when you are intent on reaching a goal, it is necessary to associate with certain people in order to reach your goal. In their company, you may be tempted to pleasures and actions that are inappropriate for the superior person. To participate in such low pleasures or actions would certainly bring remorse. At those times, you should not let yourself be enticed from the path of the superior person. Just as you should not allow yourself to be unresistingly swept along by unfavorable circumstances, neither should you allow inferior people to erode your good character.

The same advice for choosing friends holds true in the selection of a mate. There is an old saying that "love is blind."

In many ways, that is a blessing because it helps you to be tolerant of your partner. However, it is also important not to deceive yourself about the person in whom you're interested and to be observant. The I Ching describes how you can be observant:

> *If we want to know what anyone is like,*
> *we have only to observe on what he bestows*
> *his care and what sides of his own nature*
> *he cultivates and nourishes.*

Each person reveals himself by what he says and does, by the way he dresses, by the way he responds to events, by what he reads and watches, and generally by the way he lives life. By observing anyone, you can see what that person is like.

Remember as well that just as being in the presence of certain people can pull you down, being in the company of a well-intentioned friend can have a wonderfully beneficial effect upon you, particularly if you take advantage of the opportunity to improve yourself. The I Ching teaches:

> *If you see good, imitate it.*
> *If you have faults, rid yourself of them.*

That ethical attitude is the most important character attribute you can cultivate. It is one of the ways the superior person brightens his already bright virtue.

If you want to begin a friendship or relationship with someone and don't know how to proceed, turn to the I Ching for direction. You can ask:

> "What can I do to have a relationship with John/ Susan?"

In addition, it is always important to ask:

> "What can I expect from entering into a relationship with my new friend?"

Be sure to follow the I Ching's instructions and reflect deeply on the advice you receive. Following the advice you are given will save you much pain and heartbreak later. If you are not clear about the answer you receive, rephrase your question and ask again.

THE TIME OF GATHERING TOGETHER

Although the I Ching advises us to take care in entering into relationships, it also advises us to relax and have faith in the Universe:

> *In the time of gathering together,*
> *make no arbitrary choice of your associates.*
> *There are secret forces at work, leading*
> *together those who belong together.*

An arbitrary choice is one that is made on the basis of personal preference, without regard to laws or principles. This saying tells us that in the time of gathering together, the secret forces that are leading together those who belong together may bring you into association with people who are not of your personal preference but who, nonetheless, will be of great benefit.

Thus, in all relationships the I Ching counsels us to be both careful and observant as well as open-minded about who we may be drawn to and who may be drawn to us. Ultimately, if you are seeking a mate or partner, you need not fear that you will not find the right person. The Universe, which is aware of you, knows what and who you need for your growth. If indeed you are to have a partner in a relationship, exactly the right partner will be provided. What you make of the relationship once you have it is entirely in your own hands.

CHAPTER NINE

Overcoming Fear

Integrity is one of the single most important character traits you can develop. Integrity extends far beyond telling the truth. It has to do with how you perform your tasks, how you treat the people with whom you come in contact, how you respond to events, and whether or not you can be trusted. In the end, your integrity or lack of it produces the quality of your life.

We lose our integrity and our truthfulness by succumbing to fear. All lies have their basis in fear. The only reason you have ever lied is that you were afraid, and all your fears were based upon your expectations of bad results. You knew what the truth was, but you believed that if you told it, you would experience a bad consequence. If you had expected a beneficial result from telling the truth, you would have told the truth. Instead, you reshaped what had happened or was going to happen and then talked about it in a way that you hoped would trick your listeners into believing your improvised version of reality.

By doing that, did you change the reality of what happened? No, the truth still existed. You just distorted the situation and created something with which you then had to cope. Losing your integrity by succumbing to fear is a poor trade-off. In contrast, telling the truth brings you directness of mind. The waste of time and energy in planning, executing, and maintaining a lie is eliminated from your life. You enjoy straight thinking and straight talking, which takes you straight to your goals.

You can help yourself cope with fear by imagining yourself as the hero in a story. Imagine how you would want your hero to act in the situation you're faced with, imagine the rewards your hero will get for acting courageously, and then act as you would want your hero to act.

FEAR AND COURAGE

To experience fear, you must use your imagination to project a bad outcome. You can just as easily use your imagination to project a beneficial outcome. It may not always seem as if you have that choice, but you do. Ask yourself in any given situation: "Where is my fear coming from? Is my fear really inherent in the situation itself, or is it coming from my imagining what will be the outcome?"

Fear and courage go hand in hand. Fear cannot block you if you call forth courage, for courage empowers you to act. You have courage. How much? As much as is necessary to face the greatest fear you can possibly experience. By being courageous and acting truthfully in the face of your fears, you not only experience a beneficial outcome, but you also gain strength and improve your self-image. You get to feel really good about yourself.

The experiences that cause you to feel fear are actually useful to you. They are directed at your weakest areas. The experience comes to you so you can use your courage to overcome the fear, thereby strengthening your weak area. These workout situations are completely for your benefit. As a result of seeing them through courageously, not only will you strengthen yourself, but you will also gain a bonus benefit as well. You will gain a gift for having passed the test, and the gift is different each time.

In the language of the I Ching, fear as well as hope can be seen as moods:

> *To remain at the mercy of moods*
> *of hope and fear will cost you your*
> *inner composure and consistency.*

Hope contains the subtle fear that what you hope for will not come to pass. Fear contains the subtle hope that what you fear will not come to pass. Neither state is appropriate to the superior person, who turns everything to his advantage and who therefore knows that everything that occurs is for his benefit.

To remain at the mercy of hope and fear is to bob like a cork on the ocean, rising and falling as your hopes and fears assail you. You are far more powerful than you suspect, and the Universal plan includes your well-being. Therefore, have courage and faith, be joyous, and all will be well.

Exposing the Truth

The I Ching is of immense value in overcoming fear and exposing the truth. I use the phrase "exposing the truth" because whenever the cause of your fear is unmasked, there is the shining kernel of truth informing you that there is nothing that can happen to you that will not be to your great benefit. *Even the worst thing that can happen will be to your benefit.* Using the I Ching, you can ask:

"What do I need to know about my current fear?"

"What will happen if my current fear materializes?"

"What can I do to eliminate the cause of my fear?"

People have asked me, "What about the people who have AIDS or cancer or Alzheimer's who will die a painful, demoralizing death? Shouldn't they be afraid? What benefit could they possibly derive from those horrible diseases?" Those are truly difficult situations to see as being beneficial, but remember the wisdom from the I Ching that I cited in chapter one: "*That intelligent, creative, aware force [that cre-*

ated and sustains the Universe] endlessly shapes and alters us to the purpose that we will ultimately come to achieve our true nature."

Fu Hsi, the ancient Chinese sage who stated that truth so many thousands of years ago, perceived the two fundamental principles of life that are still in effect today: *"Change is constant"* and *"Every event benefits you."* When you are beginning to understand that everything that befalls you benefits you, it may be difficult to perceive that any benefit could ever come through a major catastrophe or a great illness. It is better to start practicing that philosophy with small things, like a stubbed toe, a lost wallet, or a missed bus or plane. See whether you can find a benefit in that— perhaps by realizing that stubbing your toe, for example, released an acupressure point—and then be thankful for the experience.

BENEFITING FROM FEAR AND CALAMITY

In the same way that danger provides a benefit, experiencing fear in your life can also have a beneficial effect. Fear is a warning. It is telling you that you should take action to correct the situation that is causing your fear.

As I explained earlier, when a seemingly unfortunate event befalls you, it may not always be immediately clear what the benefit is, but responding to the event or circumstance as though it were for your benefit is the magical formula that will keep you in harmony with the ever-unfolding Universe. Use the I Ching to ask:

"What is the benefit for me in the calamity I have just experienced?"

If you feel fear, ask:

"What can I expect if I face my fear?"

Whenever something happens that seems unpleasant or unlucky, your job is to say, "That was for my benefit." By responding as though what happened was for your benefit, you are working with the law of cause and effect to bring about the desired end.

CHAPTER TEN

Time, Eternity, and You

We imagine an endless future stretching out ahead of us and an endless past stretching out behind. We believe that where we exist is the moment we call "now," that this moment is a tiny hairline that separates the future from the past. The reverse is true. All there is and was and ever will be is an endless now. Is it not always now?

> *The superior person sees and understands*
> *the transitory, that which passes away,*
> *in the light of eternity.*

The superior person understands that this moment we call now is all that exists and, as such, is as much of eternity as eternity itself. He therefore understands that whatever occurs within this moment of now is perfect, just as eternity is perfect. Carrying this thought further, he understands that being part of eternity, he is perfect—and you are perfect. Anyone who completely grasps that concept will feel his sense of impermanence, his sense that life is transitory, evaporating as mist in the air.

To understand the transitory, that which passes away, see those things that pass away in the light that *every ending contains a new beginning.* Yet, even endings and beginnings are illusions. *They are simply situations and matter flowing into their various forms and conditions.*

We talk about the ending of the day and the beginning of the night, yet it is really neither of those. It is the Earth turning and showing us a view of the sun or taking that view away, giving the illusion of a beginning and an ending. What we perceive as day and night or beginning and ending are all a matter of transformation—endless transformation. What appears in matter as transitory is really only form changing. Conditions are constantly changing, flowing, merging, ending, beginning, in an endless procession. Everything in its basic form is energy and, in its essence, is eternal—including you.

"Before" and "After"

There is only one real unit of time—now. Time seems to flow onward, to progress because we age and because change occurs. We also conceive of "before" and "after" because we can't put two physical objects in the same space at the same time.

However, what our senses and our reason tell us about time is misleading. "Before" and "after" exist within the totality of time. Time is the chalkboard on which "before" and "after" write themselves. To conceive of that more easily, imagine writing a sentence on a chalkboard. Does the board unfold as you write, creating more of itself as you write each letter? No. The total board exists all the time. It is the same with time. It exists completely, all at once; and within it, change takes place.

For you to be able to hear sound, there must be silence within which the sound can be heard. For you to be able to perceive change, there must be a changelessness against which change can be seen. For you to be able to perceive movement, there must be nonmovement against which the movement can be seen. In the same way, with time there must be a "no-time," or an endless time, an "is-ness." "No-time" is the consciousness of the Universe and it pervades everything. Within that consciousness, as part of that consciousness, you exist.

In my book *A Tale of the I Ching: How the Book of Changes Began*, Fu Hsi (the Chinese sage who created the I Ching) tells his young disciple what the Void is, and he speaks of change. Their conversation follows.

Fu Hsi said, "It is time for you to enter into the Void."

"The Void? Where is that?"

"That is what I call the space where everything exists before it is formed. It is as if you had an image in your mind of a figure, and then you carved the figure out of wood. Before the wooden figure emerged, the idea of it was in your thoughts. It is the same with everything that exists; an image of everything exists in the Void before it is created, a perfect image. Do you know what a mold is?"

"Yes, Great Master. I have a shell into which I pack wet sand. Then I turn the shell upside down and tap it lightly, and then I remove the shell. The sand remains formed in the image of the shell. The shell is a mold."

"Exactly."

The disciple opened his mouth to ask whether there was a mold for himself, but then he realized that Fu Hsi had just told him that everything had a mold. So he closed his mouth and withheld his question.

Fu Hsi, who seemed to miss nothing, smiled and said, "Yes, you too have a mold."

The disciple colored a bit but recovered quickly from his small embarrassment and said, "Revered Master, do the images from which all things come change?"

Fu Hsi smiled. "Are you asking that question because you have seen that everything is always changing?"

This time the disciple had to comment, "You always seem to be able to read my thoughts. Yes, that is why I ask."

"That is a good question. The answer is that the image is fully formed, including all of its states of change, from its seeming birth to its seeming death, all at the same time."

Either End Is Magnificent

When Fu Hsi told his disciple that the images of everything are completely formed, including all their states of change, he was saying that time is one, that everything exists within "no-time," or endless time. It is like a videotape of a movie. The entire movie is there on the videotape from its beginning to its end. To experience the movie, you must play the tape. You watch as the film unfolds, yet at all times the entire film exists. It is that way with time. In the Void exist the images of everything, including all their states of change. You do not see the future unfold; you see the past unfold. By the time you perceive anything, it is already part of the past, even if it is only a billionth of a second later. That will be obvious to you if you think about it.

Our sun will, at some time billions of years in the future, become a giant red star, expanding to many times its current size. It will engulf the Earth, and our little planet will be returned to the Void. Does that mean that the human race as we know it is doomed? Perhaps. We will necessarily go through some transitions, but we will always be part of the eternal Universe, as we are now, always flowing into our various forms.

Our existence on this planet is very frail. If, for instance, a deadly virus such as the AIDS virus were to be transmitted by air rather than by blood, it would quickly destroy human life. If we continue to heat the atmosphere and the polar ice caps begin to melt, we will lose our dry land. If we continue to destroy our greenery and the ozone layer with pollutants, radiation from the sun will eventually destroy us.

Is that the end for us? No, of course not. It only means that this most beautiful planet will, at some time in the future, become uninhabitable. As for us, we will either be reabsorbed into the totality of the Universe or we will retain our individuality and appear in some other part of the Universe. I want to make something very clear here. When I write that we will be reabsorbed into the totality of the Universe, I mean only that our form will change. We are part of the Universe *now*. We cannot actually be "reabsorbed" because we are always a part of it.

Being part of the Universe, you too are eternal. Whether you keep your individuality when you die and exist on another level, another dimension, or whether you lose your individuality and merge into the totality of All-That-Is is of little consequence. Either end is magnificent.

So, relax. Be of good cheer. You are in the best of all possible hands: the hands of the Universe. That's like saying you are in your own hands, since you and the Universe are one. Remember, the Universe is here, you are here, and that makes everything possible. We were there at the beginning, *if there ever was one.* A Universe capable of creating itself can do anything and everything.

I realize this chapter opens the possibility of endless discussions about fate, free will, and chaos, but this little book is not the place for those discussions. It is enough to know that you are eternal, that by walking the path of the superior person you will soar to great heights of good fortune and success, that the Universe is alive and aware, supremely aware of you, and that you are part of it all.

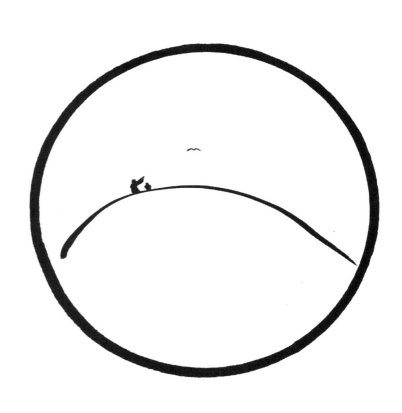

CHAPTER ELEVEN

Children

"You're wonderful, and I love you." Fortunate indeed is the child whose parents say those wonderful, stabilizing words many times during his or her childhood years. To implant that message deeply in the psyche of our children is a gift almost beyond reckoning. Whenever misfortune or setbacks occur in the child's life, whenever criticism or rejection is encountered, there are those words, feeding the child from a deep level: "You're wonderful, and I love you."

Infants are spirits, divine beings who come to earth to gain experience. Our job as parents, educators, friends, or guardians is to help children develop a good self-image and to provide them with the correct information so that they will be able to act on the basis of what is true in the Universe rather than on superstition or false beliefs.

What we learn as children sets the pattern for the rest of our days on earth. We all begin as babies with unspoiled, fresh, pure minds, free from care, free from prejudice, free from thoughts of hate, anger, and fear. The chalkboards of our minds are clear, ready to be written upon by our parents, teachers, and friends, by our experience, and by ourselves. We are ready to learn.

Parents generally think of their children as "theirs" and believe that they have the right to do with them as they see fit. Some parents feel that the child is a burden, an unwelcome obligation; others feel blessed. Fortunate is the child whose parents understand their true roles: teachers, guides, protectors, providers.

Even more fortunate is the child whose parents understand that they and their child are spiritually connected, that their association goes back to the beginning of the Universe, and that they have come to this planet in advance of the child to pave the way, to lead the child into a correct understanding of his mission here on earth and his relationship to the Universe. I know of no more important information that a child can receive than that the Universe is alive and aware, reacting to the child's every state of being, every thought, and every action, and that the child is a part of that Universe, an inseparable, eternal, glorious part.

THE PERFECT CONDITIONS FOR GROWTH

We may have forgotten how we came to earth, but however we got here, the circumstances were exactly right for each of us. That is vitally important for our children to know if they are to lead great lives. All developing souls require growth in particular areas of their soul life, and the circumstances into which each of us is born provide perfectly for that growth—no exceptions.

It is not only useless for you to lament the circumstances into which you were born and the conditions under which you were raised, but it is also detrimental to your growth as an individual and a sign of unawareness. No matter the circumstances of your childhood, no matter the care or lack of it that you received from your parents, no matter the abundance or lack of it in your home, no matter what experiences you suffered, your job now is to be grateful for whatever it took to bring you to this moment in time. Whatever those circumstances were, they were perfect for you, as they are for each of us.

In fact, the very circumstances that you lament are the most important and powerful events of your life. It is from those events that you will discover your future power and gain the wisdom and information you need to grow. You get very little from the humdrum existence of daily life. It is the powerful experiences that provide the opportunities to grow, to mature, and to learn. It is those experiences that you must treasure. The beating, the abandonment, the deprivation, the rape, the trauma are all there for your benefit. If you fail to understand that, you will lament those incidences for the rest of your life.

Rather than letting those seemingly unfortunate experiences burden you and weigh you down, see them as springboards from which you can vault to the skies of success. Adversity is for your strengthening. Where would the body builder be without the weights? A diamond is polished by grit and a human by adversity. Welcome the challenges that come into your life; see them as workout situations.

A Change in Outlook

To feel deprived, cheated, unfortunate, or ill-used as a result of your childhood circumstances is to declare yourself unaware of the essential need for the very circumstances into which you were born and under which you were raised. Carrying such a burden and thinking of yourself as a victim colors all the days of your life a dull gray. It spoils the singing of the lark. We must teach our children to see the opportunity for growth and change in their circumstances, no matter how rich or poor those circumstances may be, and we must teach them the necessity for having experienced those circumstances.

As soon as you change your perception from viewing events of the past or present as burdensome or unlucky to viewing them as beneficial situations from which you will gain power, wisdom, and information, the world will immediately seem a different place. The choice of how you see events is completely up to you. Take this moment to resolve to change the way you see all events. Teach your children to do the same.

Of course, we all want to better the circumstances in which we find ourselves. By bettering our circumstances, we gain strength, expand our awareness, and benefit from living in a better environment. Just remember that no matter what circumstances you have or are experiencing, the opportunity for improvement is always there. In fact, when the opportunity for improvement is no longer in your life, you will cease to exist on this level. Here's a test you can use to see if you've finished improving yourself: If you're alive, you're not finished.

So if you feel you have been a victim of circumstances, free yourself of that burden now. Use the I Ching and the yarrow stalks to ask why you have experienced what you have and to discover why you needed to have the experiences that caused you pain.

It is very difficult to make the change from feeling victimized to feeling grateful for whatever has occurred in your life, but you must do so if you are to see all occurrences in their proper light. Once you have accomplished that goal, you will then respond to new events in a way that sweeps away all obstacles before you, leaving your road clear and the wind fair. That major change in outlook will bring you the rewards of supreme good fortune and great success.

That is the main lesson you must teach your children. Seemingly unfortunate events will befall them; it is part of the human condition. It is how they view those events that will determine the outcome of those events in their lives.

Exercising Power

The guidance the I Ching provides on the use and misuse of power can also guide us in caring for children. For instance, the I Ching counsels:

> *Power best expresses itself*
> *in gentleness.*

The bully, the despot, and the person in authority who uses his power to hurt others are all universally disliked. They create their own unpleasant environment within which they must exist. By contrast, the superior person in a position of power can be clearly recognized by his gentleness. His gentle expression of power does not provoke resentment or incur resistance and so makes the attainment of his purposes and the continued growth of his power easy. By following the example of the superior person, you will go your way unopposed on a smooth, easy road.

Those same principles apply to parenthood. For our children to become healthy-minded, strong adults, we must carefully nurture them. Hitting children or screaming at them is absolutely to be avoided. Such acts not only deaden the child's sensitivity, but they also cause the child to lose respect for the parent and destroy the possibility of any real closeness or communication between parent and child. The old maxim "spare the rod and spoil the child" is barbaric. Respect is not to be confused with fear. Hitting a child may induce fear, but respect can never be gained in that way.

When the power a parent has over a child is used incorrectly, the child develops in a warped manner. While it is true that whatever a child experiences will eventually serve his or her best interests, provide opportunities for growth, and make the child stronger, an aware parent only uses power to act for the child, never against the child.

In all situations, those of us who would like to use the power we wield to enrich ourselves and those around us must be certain only to exercise that power for the highest and best interests of everyone. The I Ching also advises:

> *For power to be truly great, it must remain*
> *inwardly united with the fundamental*
> *principles of right and justice.*

The inferior person, concerned only for his own well-being and pleasure, uses his power to further his own selfish ends and to cause hurt and trouble for others. This is the degenerative use of power and bodes ill for everyone, particularly the wielder of the power. The superior person, concerned with the principles of right and justice, uses his power to aid others and improve the general welfare. This bodes well for everyone, particularly the wielder of the power.

Raising Spirited Children

Because parents are stronger, quicker, and better informed than their young children, they can always win in a given situation with their children. However, if you want your children to develop into winners, you must provide them with the experience of winning when they are children.

In little foot races, in discussions, in willpower struggles, and in many other ways, the child should be allowed to win. That course of action may have a tendency to make the child more difficult to handle, but if you want to raise children to be like fiery steeds rather than the spiritless horses that are used to pull milk carts, you must allow them to win.

Likewise, a child should be encouraged to reason with a parent. If you forbid a child to do something and the child then questions your decision or fights against it, it is easy for you to powerfully overcome the child's protests. Yet, failing to encourage the child to fight for what he wants may erode the child's will and program him or her to accept the dictates of others without question. As a result, the child may fail to stand up for his or her rights later in life.

Parents often tell their children, "Do what I tell you to do," and later, "Do what the teacher tells you to do," and again, "Do what the babysitter tells you to do." Fairly soon, the child does what everyone tells him to do, and we later wonder why our children did not grow into strong, independent people.

Encouraging your children to develop a strong, winning spirit does not, however, mean you should pamper them. The I Ching teaches:

> *If one clings to the little boy,*
> *one loses the strong man.*

There is a point in each person's life when he must leave behind childish ideas and the need to cling to an adult if he is to become a strong, independent person. If, as a parent, you pamper your children, you will prevent them from becoming strong and independent and you will prevent them from gaining strength on their own. If you always carry your children, they will never develop their own muscles to walk and run. Sometimes a generous, loving parent is the most difficult hurdle a developing child has to overcome, for a parent's desire to nurture can lead to indulgence.

Throughout the life of your children, you will be called upon to play a variety of roles and take a variety of actions, and these actions may differ depending on the circumstance and the child involved. Using your divinatory powers to access the I Ching for direction is one of the best ways to gain information about bringing up children and to understand what to do in various circumstances. You can ask questions such as:

"What can I expect from enrolling my child in Forest Hills school?"

"How will the new neighborhood affect my children?"

"What can my daughter expect from a career as a doctor?"

"How can my son solve his problem in school?"

"How can I improve myself as a parent?"

"How can I improve my relationship with my daughter?"

"What counsel should I give my son regarding his current problem?"

THE REASONS YOU ARE HERE

In the hustle and bustle of earning a living and sorting out the day-to-day problems associated with life, you can become caught up in the whirl of the senses and the press of the problems, forgetting your true mission. You can forget the reasons you are here on earth—to gain experience, to perfect yourself as a divine being, and to impart that knowledge to your children.

How do you perfect yourself? Keep aware of your mission. All else will occur as a result of natural law. The difference between living life aware or not aware of your mission is as dramatic as the difference between night and day. It is the difference between going through life with All-That-Is as a knowing, cooperative, helping partner and going through life alone in a seemingly inert, dead, unresponsive Universe. I say "seemingly" because the Universe is not inert, dead, or unresponsive, but if you are unaware of the life of the Universe, of its consciousness, you will not consciously communicate with and interact with the Universe. Neither will you be aware of the subtle promptings of the Universe or understand that the events occurring in your life are Universal occurrences that are there for your benefit.

TRUST BUILDS A STRONG RELATIONSHIP

One of the most important messages you can give your children is "You can do it." Self-confidence gives children the power to accomplish goals, to overcome fears, and to become who and what they want to become. With that goal in mind, you should encourage your children to take on ever-greater tasks and ever-greater responsibility, instilling in them the confidence that they can accomplish their goals.

Another way to build self-confidence in children is to trust them. Trust builds the child's self-respect and causes the child to respect you. You should also trust your child's judgment. By doing that, you will teach a child self-reliance. Children want us to trust them and have confidence in them. Indeed, it is one of their most sought-after goals. You build their morale when you extend to them your trust and confidence. It makes them feel important, loved, and dependable.

In addition, try not to be overly critical of your children. They want you to see them as strong, capable, and reliable. If you firmly hold that image of your children in your mind, as a process of natural law they will surely fulfill that image. Hold that image no matter what befalls them, no matter if you are disappointed in them, no matter what they do, no matter what they say. As a result, your relationships with your children will be strong and lasting.

CHAPTER TWELVE

Work

One of the most wonderful blessings that can befall any of us is to be able to earn a living doing what we love. Yet work is often thought of and spoken of as a distasteful chore, something we must do to earn money, to keep our homes clean, to take care of ourselves and others, to buy clothing and other essentials, and to provide ourselves with the wherewithal to have fun.

Many of us are either bound to a job we don't like by circumstances we believe to be insurmountable or we believe we are unsuited by education, opportunity, or talent to work in a field that would please us. The truth is that you are not bound to work that you dislike because of circumstances or lack of opportunity, talent, or education—you are bound by your beliefs. You can change any of the circumstances of your life, work included, *but only if you believe you can change them*. If you don't believe you can, you won't even make the attempt.

By far, most of the people I have met in my lifetime were working at jobs they did not particularly like and, in some cases, actually hated. The reason each person gave for not choosing to do something else was different, but, in essence, the reasons were all the same: fear. They feared loss of income, loss of seniority, not being able to find another job, or some similar condition. The reasons were endless, but they were all based on fear. And, of course, the people didn't believe they could make the desired changes.

FEAR AND LACK OF CONFIDENCE

The fear that makes us hold on to something that sustains us before we have something else to take its place stems from lack of confidence—lack of confidence in ourselves or lack of confidence in the Universe of which we are a part. One of the major discoveries of my life has been that if we trust the Universe and *act on the basis of that trust*, we will not only achieve our goals but, for having acted out of trust in the Universe, we will also receive the bonus benefit I mentioned earlier—a gift for having passed the test.

If you are in a work situation that is less than satisfying, resolve now to change it. Remember that you are part of a glorious Universe that wants you to have the best of everything. If you fail to act on the basis of that belief, you are not living up to your potential as a great human being.

When you have questions or concerns about the right course of action to take in a situation related to your job or career, you can make wonderful use of the I Ching and yarrow stalks by asking questions such as:

> "How can I get to do the work I love?"

> "What will happen if I leave my present employment and seek work elsewhere?"

> "What can I expect if I start my own business?"

> "What can I expect if I switch jobs?"

> "How can I earn more money?"

> "What can I do to improve myself so I can earn more money?"

> "How can I get ahead in my company?"

> "What do I need to know about my job?"

> "What can I expect if I seek work in another part of the state?"

> "What will happen if I ask for a raise?"

> "What will happen if I go over the head of my superior and complain about his poor work habits?"

> "What can I expect if I remain with my present employer?"

Do Every Task for Its Own Sake

One of the most important principles for achieving success in work is to do each task for its own sake, without regard to the reward you will receive for completing the task. The

I Ching advises:

> *Do not set your eyes on the harvest*
> *while planting it, nor on the use of*
> *the ground while clearing it.*

Every task must receive the attention it deserves if it is to turn out well. Anticipating the outcome of your efforts may cause you to become impatient and overeager, and you may hurry to complete the task. Hasty or careless work will result in unsatisfactory performance of the task, which, of course, will bring about an unsatisfactory result. Do every task for its own sake and do it as well as you can, and it will naturally follow that you will achieve good fortune and great success.

In addition, do not complain that your work is tedious or that you are doing more than another or being paid less or that your employer doesn't care for the employees. Whatever your work is, do it to the best of your ability, as if you were doing it for yourself, for your own benefit. You are a child of the Universe. If you are generous with yourself and your time, by virtue of the Universal law of cause and effect you will be amply rewarded. If you hold back giving your efforts or your time, the Universal law of cause and effect will take its toll.

Many of us desire to get ahead in the workplace, to be in a position of leadership. By focusing your attention on doing each task that is assigned to you to the utmost of your ability and by fulfilling your duties conscientiously, you will rapidly achieve your goals as a consequence of natural law. Giving generously of your efforts and your time and relying on the Universe to reward you will cause you to move upward through the ranks as though drawn by six strong horses.

MOTIVATION AND SERVICE

Before striving to rise to a position of leadership, you are wise to ask yourself what is your motivation for wanting to do so. Most likely, it is the additional income you will receive for taking on added responsibility. Also, a rise in position will usually give you more freedom and respect within the workplace. However, there are other reasons for rising to a position of leadership that will serve you well if you know of them and aspire to them. The I Ching tells us:

> *If you would rule,*
> *first learn to serve.*

The only valid reason for a superior person to want to rule is so he can better serve those he rules. If you are unprepared or unwilling to serve your followers, it is better for them and for you that you never achieve rulership, because if you do and then cease to serve them, you will lose your following. All your efforts will have been for naught and you will suffer great embarrassment. By first learning to serve, you will come to understand those who will eventually serve you. Only through serving can you obtain from those you rule the joyous assent that is necessary if they are to follow you.

In situations where you are considering a leadership position, you can use the I Ching to ask questions such as:

"What can I expect from taking on a position of leadership?"

"What do I need to know about leading my fellow workers?"

Once you are in a position of power, find a use for everyone and everything. In this way, you will be loved and respected and your power will blossom, carrying you to ever-greater heights. The I Ching teaches:

In the hands of a great master,
all material is productive.

A great master wastes nothing; therefore, he always has enough. He values everyone; therefore, everyone values him.

CHAPTER THIRTEEN

Gain and Loss

The way you view gains, losses, and the unfolding of events in your life is critical to your success and your happiness. *You are not your gain; neither are you your loss.* The I Ching teaches:

> *Take not gain or loss to heart.*
> *What man holds high comes to nothing.*

Gain and loss are external to you, things with which your eternal soul is not concerned. All gains and losses pass away at the time of death. Do not waste even a moment on gains and losses when death is plucking your ears, saying, "Live! I am coming."

In order to put your gains and losses in perspective and use them both to your best advantage, consider the following saying of the I Ching:

> *A situation only becomes favorable*
> *when one adapts to it.*

All events are for your complete advantage from the moment they occur, although it may not seem that way in the beginning. Events are simply events; the way you respond to events determines their final outcome in your life. As long as you are angry or upset over a situation or an event, you will be unable to perceive its beneficial aspects, and you may wear yourself out with unnecessary resistance.

YOU ARE IN CHARGE OF THE WAY YOU FEEL

You are in charge of the way you feel about things. At times, you may not control your reactions to events. You may react on the spur of the moment without thinking; you may react out of hurt, fear, or surprise or out of indignation or pride.

Once an event has taken place, all that is left to you is your response. Why not respond as though the event occurred for your benefit? If you do so, you will immediately experience good feelings about the event, and by acting in accord with your feelings, you will help to bring about that end.

Remember: *You are part of the Universe.*

Remember: *The Universe is well inclined, beneficially inclined.*

Remember: *Everything that happens will ultimately benefit you.*

Remembering those things will cause you to react to the ever-unfolding events of the Universe in a positive manner, which, in itself, is already a benefit and will bring you good fortune and great success. If you sustain a loss or experience a hurtful occurrence, it is also well to keep in mind what is still left to you. The I Ching advises:

> *Do not complain.*
> *Enjoy the good fortune*
> *you still possess.*

While the inferior person bitterly complains and curses his luck when faced with an undesirable situation or confronted with a loss, the superior person remembers the good things still left to him and smiles. He knows that happy turns of fortune sometimes come in a form that at first seems strange or unlucky, and therefore he realizes that seemingly undesirable situations or losses will ultimately be a benefit to him. Thus, he responds in a positive way. The inferior person is sad; the superior person is glad. Each is in charge of his response. Each has set the pattern for the continuing course of events.

REMAIN TRUE TO YOURSELF

On life's path, great riches or enticements may dazzle you and may cause you to attempt to get them by means that are inappropriate to the superior person. Such actions always lead to remorse. According to the I Ching, no matter what enticements come your way, it is always best to remain true to yourself.

If you are not dazzled by enticing goals,
and remain true to yourself, you will travel
through life unassailed, on a level road.

If you remain true to yourself, if you live up to the best within yourself, you will always walk the path of the superior person and, in so doing, reap the rewards of a prince and the glory of a king. The rewards of a prince and the glory of a king are truly wonderful gifts, and I do not use those phrases lightly. Everything you read here is deliberately written and is meant to be taken literally. The rewards of a prince and the glory of a king are not necessarily material things, although they may be. There are greater things to be sought after than material things. After all, in time all material objects become nothing. Everything, the moment it is made, begins to decay. Is it wise, therefore, to set much store in finery and other such objects? The I Ching tells us:

Even the finest clothes
turn to rags.

The superior person does not attach great importance to things that decay. He does attach great importance to things that endure: his integrity, his honor, his virtue, and his appreciation and reverence for All-That-Is. That is not to say that you should not value your possessions, for they can bring you much pleasure; but you should not set great store by them, for they are transitory, and there are other, greater treasures.

You have already received the greatest gift of all—*you are part of this glorious Universe.* In light of that, *everything else is inconsequential.* If you look at events in the context of "right here and right now," you may see yourself as sustaining losses, being hurt, rejected, ill-used, or unlucky. But if you look at those losses or occurrences in the context of eternity, which is how long you'll be part of the Universe, you'll see that those things are truly inconsequential. In the context of eternity, all of this lifetime is less than one trillionth of the beat of a hummingbird's wing. Your job is to see the things that cause you distress as being for your ultimate benefit and to deal with them in that way.

When faced with circumstances of gain or loss, you can use the I Ching to inquire:

"Why am I experiencing this seemingly unpleasant situation?"

"How can I best deal with this turn of events?"

If in the past you were led to do things that were not in keeping with the actions of a superior person, before taking those kinds of actions again, you can simply ask:

"What can I expect from taking that action?"

Consider carefully the advice you receive before moving

ahead. Remember: *On your way to perfecting yourself as a divine being, all the material gains and losses you experience are of no more consequence than the flutter of an eyelash.* The way you handle them is of great consequence, for it is the mark of your spiritual progress or lack of it. The Universe is an ever-changing, ever-nurturing Being, and your gains and losses are part of the beneficial fluctuation of the Universe.

CHAPTER FOURTEEN

Recovery

What is recovery if not the return to health after sickness, the return to strength after weakness, a regaining of balance after imbalance, a return to wholeness after impairment, the return of a possession after a loss, the return of hope after a time of despair, the return of love after a time of its absence, the return of joy after sorrow, the return to the path of the superior person after having strayed from that path?

All decrease is followed by increase, all loss by gain, and all sorrow by joy. That is the way. The I Ching says:

Every ending contains a new beginning.

Kua 24, Fu (Return) represents the natural cycle of recovery. The kua Fu is made up of five broken lines over one solid line ䷗. In every kua of the I Ching, the lines enter from the bottom, move upward through the six stages of change (see page 11), and leave again at the top. They show the natural sequence of all things as they move from their beginnings to their endings, flowing from one condition to another. The kua describes situations, conditions, and even life itself as it moves from a state where it is about to begin to its natural ending. That "ending" is like walking through a doorway from one room to another; it's just another transformation and as completely natural as birth.

What are called broken lines in any kua represent the dark force, or the weak force. The solid lines represent the light force, the powerful force. Kua 24 shows a light force line (a solid line) entering from the bottom. The five broken lines above that solid line tell us that prior to that new line entering from the bottom, all the lines were dark force lines, representing a time of darkness. A solid line entering from the bottom signifies a return of the light force.

Everything Turns toward Its Opposite

The kua Fu (Return) could also be called Recovery because of its meaning. It signifies that after all periods of darkness comes a time of light, that after all despair comes hope, that after all loss comes gain. There is always renewal, as the I Ching explains:

> *No plain not followed by a slope,*
> *no increase not followed by a decrease.*

It is an eternal law of the Universe that *everything turns toward its opposite when it reaches its maximum potential.* Knowing that law, the superior person provides for a time of decrease in times of prosperity. He builds himself up during times of good health and so prepares against a time of illness. In times of safety, he takes precautions that will protect him in times of danger. He thinks ahead and, in so doing, is prepared. He thereby enjoys a lifetime of good fortune and success.

We can even look at the loss of those we love in the context of this natural cycle of increase and decrease. All of us who lose a loved one are but a half step away from following that loved one ourselves. As I said earlier, there are only two possibilities open to us when our time here on earth is over. We either retain our individuality and continue evolving or we are absorbed into the totality of the Universe. *Either end is magnificent.* We are actually never apart from the Universe at any time. Separation, in the Universal sense of the word, is an impossibility.

During your remaining time on earth, keep a bright outlook. Be cheerful. The Universe would not crown this wonderful life with a bad ending. To learn more about your life cycle, you can use the I Ching to ask:

"What can I expect after I pass on from this life?"

ONE STEP AT A TIME

The I Ching says that we should keep in mind at all times that everything changes and transforms. It also says that when we are waiting for a situation to transform itself, we should not be merely hoping or worrying, but we should be filled with certainty.

> *Waiting should not be mere empty hoping;*
> *it should be filled with the inner*
> *certainty of reaching the goal.*

If you are uncertain about reaching your goal, your waiting will be filled with worrying and fearful imaginings, both of which are detrimental to productivity and lead away from success. If, instead, you are certain of reaching your goal, your waiting will be filled with happy thoughts and useful occupation, both of which lead directly to success.

Take one step at a time. Even the longest journey starts with only the first step. No matter how poor your personal circumstances, the path of the superior person—which only leads to supreme good fortune and great success—is always directly in front of you. *You may take the first step upon it at any time and magically transform your circumstances.* These benefits are available to everyone, withheld from no one.

At all times, the path of the inferior person is also directly in front of you, bringing its lessons of hardship, misery, and despair, but only so that you will ultimately come to know the truth. At each step of your way, you must choose between those two paths. The ending of one path always means the beginning of the other. Choose well; your future is entirely in your own hands.

CHAPTER FIFTEEN

Health

Whenever you meet someone who has obvious good health, he or she almost always has a cheerful countenance and a good outlook on life. If you were to ask the next hundred people you meet what is the most important thing in life, good health would always be near the top, if not *at* the top. If the person you ask is in poor health, it will always be *at* the top of that person's list.

Good health mainly comes from the thoughts you hold in your mind. The I Ching maintains that a healthy body is the product of a healthy mind:

> *Those things in your psychic body*
> *later manifest in your physical body.*

The mind is a creator, and what you hold there manifests itself in one way or another. If worry and stress occupy your mind, they will manifest themselves in your body as tension and pain. If you hold thankfulness and joy in your mind, they will manifest themselves in your body as radiant health and a shining countenance.

Your habits also play a crucial role in maintaining abundant good health. Cleanliness, for instance, plays a key part in keeping healthy and it actually influences your state of mind. Whether or not you realize it, you are powerfully influenced by your surroundings. Keeping your environment neat and orderly causes a healthy condition to exist in your mind and therefore in your body. It's like a reflection; the condition of your mind is a reflection of what's taking place in your environment. The opposite is also true: *The way you keep yourself and your surroundings is a direct result, a reflection, of what goes on inside your mind.*

Cultivating Good Habits and Intentions

In essence, your surroundings affect your mind just as your mind affects your surroundings. Knowing that, you can reap the great rewards that come from adopting habits of cleanliness and neatness. As with all good habits that you cultivate, if you train yourself to be personally clean and to keep the environment in which you live and work clean, it becomes almost effortless to maintain a state of cleanliness.

It takes strength and determination to rid yourself of bad habits that control you, but by eliminating those habits you gain control, increase your strength, and have a better life. If you are too weak to overcome habits that are obviously bad for you, your future is indeed bleak. While temporary pleasures may accompany bad habits, they are detrimental to you in the long run, and they will weaken you even in the short run. Acquiring a long-term problem in exchange for a short-term pleasure is not a good bargain.

The I Ching tells us that a superior person is always in control of his habits. Yet it also says that to be successful in rooting out bad habits, it is wise to tolerate harmless habits for a time. If you are too strict with yourself, you may fail in your purpose.

> *In cultivating oneself,*
> *it is best to root out bad habits and*
> *tolerate those that are harmless.*

Good intentions, like good habits, are of tremendous benefit. All your acts are a product of your intentions. Therefore, if you have taken the time to cultivate good intentions, your acts will reflect those good intentions. The I Ching says:

> *To be a superior person, see to it that goodness*
> *is an established attribute of character rather than*
> *an accidental and isolated occurrence.*

True goodness means that your intentions are always beneficial, never hurtful. To maintain your beneficial intentions, it is necessary to renew your determination every day to follow the path of the superior person, always working to improve your character. For persevering in your efforts, you will find within yourself a wellspring of joy that will refresh and renew you all of your days.

REST AND COMPOSURE

To have good health, it is also essential to alternate periods of activity with periods of rest. The I Ching warns:

> *If you live in a state of perpetual hurry,*
> *you will fail to attain inner composure.*

Inner composure means having a settled state of mind—the qualities of calmness and tranquility. By attaining that state, you are able to act without stress and will therefore make no mistakes. In contrast, constant hurrying wears you down, destroys calmness, and puts lines in your face. Perpetual hurry upsets your inner composure and your good judgment. By slowing yourself and nurturing yourself with the ways of the superior person, all else will be achieved through the process of natural law.

In order to nurture yourself, recognize that everyone has individual needs and that those needs change throughout your life. You can use the I Ching as a guide to help you achieve good health by asking questions such as:

"What can I do to achieve optimal health?"

"How can I overcome my current illness?"

"What can I expect if I become a vegetarian?"

"What can I expect if I stop being a vegetarian?"

"What should I be paying attention to now with regard to my health?"

"How will a move to a drier climate affect my health?"

"How is my current relationship affecting my health?"

"What will happen if I continue my habit of smoking cigarettes?"

"How can I overcome my habit of eating too much?"

All the answers are at your disposal. By asking sincerely and with reverence, everything you need to live a healthy life and a life in alignment with your authentic self will be revealed to you.

CHAPTER SIXTEEN

Business

To engage in business is to work for a profit. This chapter deals with those who are "in business," meaning those who have undertaken an endeavor in the hope of earning a profit, even if it is in the employ of another.

Of course, the most important aspect of succeeding in business has to do with your character. While the opportunities to achieve success are endless, even the finest opportunity in the wrong hands comes to nothing. If your character is flawed, either your enterprises are doomed to failure or the profits from the business will in some way work against you. You will not be able to enjoy your business but will encounter endless problems. The problems may seem to be caused by outside influences, but that is not the case. *You constantly affect everything and everyone around you by being the way you are at every moment.*

The I Ching maintains that developing our character is the work of a lifetime:

The superior person spends a lifetime
developing strong character, and so enjoys a lifetime
of supreme good fortune and great success.

A tree on a mountain develops slowly, according to the law of its being, and consequently stands firmly rooted. Similarly, the development of one's character must undergo gradual development if it is to have a broad, stable base. The very gradualness of character development makes it necessary to also have perseverance so that slow progress will not become stagnation.

PERSEVERANCE

In all ventures, there is one constant and only one constant: you. People come and go, events transpire and pass away, and everything concerning your ventures changes, but you alone remain. Therefore, *you must be able to depend on yourself if you are to succeed.* Even though you may be just starting in business with little or no expertise and little or no capital, you can succeed by following the wisdom in the I Ching. This great book of wisdom advises:

You can succeed in life, no matter your
circumstances, provided you have determination
and follow the path of the superior person.

That saying tells us that all that is necessary to achieve

great success is to cultivate perseverance as an established trait of character and to follow the path of the superior person. By accomplishing those intentions, you will speed to your success as an eagle in flight.

Of course, it helps to be smart, too, but even people who aren't smart can succeed. It does not take intelligence; *it takes living the I Ching life, a life lived in harmony with the ways of the Universe.* And it does not take intelligence to get answers from the Universe through the I Ching or to follow its direction; it only takes sincerity and reverence. Anyone who approaches his questioning with sincerity and reverence will get correct answers that are entirely in his or her best interest.

There are many ways you can use the I Ching in business. For instance, before you undertake a business venture you can ask:

"What aspect of my character needs developing so I can be successful in business?"

"What can I expect from this new business venture?"

"What will happen if I take a partner?"

"What can I expect from this merger?"

"What can I expect from taking on this new product line?"

"What do I have to be careful of in this new venture?"

"Will I be successful in this business?"

"What will be the result if I apply for a business loan?"

"What can I expect if I move my business to another location?"

"What can I expect if I expand my business?"

MODESTY AND CONSCIENTIOUSNESS

Modesty and conscientiousness play a major role in business, particularly when you are just starting. Being modest means that you have cultivated a humble attitude. It means you do not give yourself airs or strut around trying to impress people, nor are you boastful of your accomplishments. The I Ching says:

> *Exceptional modesty and conscientiousness*
> *are sure to be rewarded with great*
> *success and good fortune*

Being conscientious means that you fulfill your tasks and obligations with great care. If you are exceptionally modest and conscientious while you hold a high position, your radiance will be like the sun at midday and no blame will attach to your progress. The attainment of your goals will be rapid and easy. If you are exceptionally modest and conscientious while you hold a low position, you will be recognized and rewarded, and you will rise quickly through the ranks.

As you progress, do not forget one of the most important Universal laws: *Everything turns toward its opposite when it reaches its maximum potential.* Therefore, as you near the pinnacle of your success, stay alert. The I Ching counsels:

> *On the road to success, as you near*
> *the attainment of your goal, beware of*
> *becoming intoxicated with your achievement.*

If you allow yourself to become overly excited about an approaching success, you may become careless or light-headed, fail to pay attention to crucial matters, and thereby ruin your success. It is precisely at the point of success that you must remain sober and cautious. By maintaining the attitude and course of action that brought you to the point of success, you will surely and safely arrive at your goals.

During your entire business life, do not hesitate to use your higher powers to consult with All-That-Is to find the best course of action. Even when your business is flourishing, you should ask:

> "Is there anything I should be paying attention to
> now?"

Unforeseen danger may be approaching. Using the I Ching can alert you to the danger and help you either prepare for it or avert it completely.

PLANNING, ACTION, AND FLEXIBILITY

Being conscientious also includes engaging in proper planning. When you first start in business, it is essential to have a plan. As you progress, it may be necessary to modify the plan in the face of unforeseen circumstances, but to begin without a clear plan is to invite disaster. The I Ching warns:

> *Exceptional enterprises cannot succeed*
> *unless the utmost caution is*
> *observed in their beginnings.*

In the beginning of even small undertakings, exceptional care must be exercised if your planting is to lead to flowering. How much more, then, should exceptional care be exercised when great or dangerous undertakings are begun? *A flaw built into the beginning increases with time and will ultimately cause the failure of the enterprise if not corrected.* The superior person can always see the end in the beginning; he knows the seeds. The seeds are the actions and precautions taken, or the lack of them, at the beginning of an enterprise.

While planning is imperative, the I Ching also advises that being overly cautious or rigid can lead to failure:

> *After a matter has been thoroughly considered,*
> *it is essential to form a decision and to act.*

While you are in business, you will be called upon to make many decisions. Using the I Ching to inquire about a correct course of action is of inestimable benefit. However, once you have made your inquiry and carefully considered your options, be sure to act. Opportunities have often been lost through inaction.

Reflecting and pondering must not be carried too far lest they cripple the power of decision. When the time for action has come, the moment must be seized. Once a matter has been thoroughly considered, anxious hesitation is a mistake that is bound to bring disaster because you will have missed your opportunity.

In addition, because the world and all that is in it is constantly changing, in order to be successful, you too must change. The I Ching teaches:

> *To be successful, do not be rigid and immobile*
> *in your thinking, but always keep abreast*
> *of the time and change with it.*

The Universal law that provides for constant change is the only thing in the Universe that does not change. To remain inflexible when all else is changing is to invite disaster. While it is essential to your success that you set firm courses and that you are stable enough in your character not to waver with every passing fad, it is equally essential to be aware of changing conditions and to be open and flexible enough in your thinking to change with them. Maintaining rigidity leads to failure; remaining flexible leads to success.

CONFLICT

Whenever you are engaged in earning money, you deal with people. Therefore, a successful person necessarily deals successfully with people. Being in business as an owner or an employee almost inevitably means we will encounter conflict—conflict with fellow workers, business competitors, and others with whom we transact business. In times of such conflict, says the I Ching, it is always better to settle the argument quickly and proceed to more productive affairs than to continue the conflict.

> *When entangled in a conflict, it is wise to remain*
> *so clearheaded and strong that you are always*
> *ready to come to terms with your opponent*
> *by meeting him halfway.*

In times of conflict, you are always in danger because your opponent may seek to harm or take advantage of you. Taking an opportunity to end the conflict by meeting opponents halfway, or even more than halfway, leads away from a time of conflict to a time of security. That is a wise and sensible course of action, and *the superior person seizes the opportunity, knowing that, in truth, he has won a great victory.* He knows that to carry on a conflict to the bitter end will have evil effects since the enmity will continue even if the conflict is won.

The I Ching also speaks of the wisdom of retreating under certain circumstances:

> *When confronted with insurmountable*
> *forces, retreat is proper.*

If you find yourself embroiled in a conflict with an adversary who is far stronger than you, you should not use up all your resources fighting a battle that you have only a poor chance of winning. When unable to negotiate a settlement, withdraw.

By persisting in fighting a battle that is beyond your capabilities, you risk depleting your resources so greatly that you will not be able to recover. To retreat does not mean to give up the battle. On the contrary, retreating preserves your resources and allows you time to regain your strength, renew your forces, and make new plans. When appropriate, a retreat actually makes possible a countermovement. That, in turn, makes success possible.

CHAPTER SEVENTEEN

Wealth

It takes great wisdom to handle wealth correctly. Once you have achieved your wealth, you must act wisely or the same laws that brought your wealth to you will remove it from you. The wisdom of the I Ching can assist you in both preserving and increasing your abundance.

As I noted earlier, because of the Universal law of increase and decrease, one following the other, the I Ching advises that it is wise to prepare for a time of decrease when you are still in a time of increase. The I Ching also explains that how you treat those with whom you interact will directly impact your wealth.

For instance, in the normal course of events, you will encounter ineptitude, carelessness, or even deliberate violations on the part of people who are in your employ, with whom you are associated, or with whom you are transacting business. If you take these people to task for their actions, you risk disturbing the successful upward spiral of your business affairs. In cases like this, the I Ching advises:

In times of prosperity, it is important
to possess enough greatness of spirit
to bear with the mistakes of others.

Just as water washes everything clean, the superior person pardons mistakes and forgives even intentional violations. In that way, he insures the upward spiral of his prosperity. The inferior person cannot resist the opportunity to chastise another and, in so doing, incurs resentment, destroys unanimity, and crushes enthusiasm, thereby destroying his own chances for success. Of course, there are times when it is necessary to reprimand someone or even terminate your association with someone, but you should give careful thought to such actions before taking them.

Simplicity

To preserve wealth, it is also essential to be thrifty. The wisdom of the I Ching cautions us not to overspend.

In financial matters,
well-being prevails when expenditures
and income are in proportion.

In short, out of debt, out of danger. It is not wise to spend more than you have, for improper use of credit enslaves. In addition, if you always spend all that you have, you will be unprepared in times of decline or emergency. Such poor planning leads to the destruction of well-being and invites disaster.

In keeping with the advice of the I Ching to keep expenditures and income in proportion, it is nearly always prudent to cut back on expenditures. Cutting back on expenditures may cause you to appear miserly, selfish, or poor, and while that feeling might make you uncomfortable, it may be necessary to preserve what you have. The I Ching further states:

Do not be ashamed
of simplicity or small means.

Simplicity is the hallmark of the superior person, while ostentation is the hallmark of the inferior person. If you are following the path of the superior person, you understand that you are the equal of any person on earth. There is no need, therefore, to present false appearances. Even with slender means or no means at all, you can express the sentiments of your heart. In reality, it is not for the monetary value of your gifts that you are appreciated but for the sentiments with which you give them.

GENEROSITY AND DISCRIMINATION

People who are in need often approach those who are wealthy for help. If you indiscriminately give to all who ask, you will shortly be without wealth yourself. Therefore, it is wise to take each case separately and to look deeply into each situation before deciding on a course of action. Rarely is it a good course of action to give money to someone who has not earned it. It will more than likely hurt that person rather than help him. Unearned wealth is nearly always a burden and leads unerringly to the detriment of those to whom it is given.

Setting up a trust to provide income for your children, for instance, is a great error. It deprives them of the incentive to work; and without engaging in some meaningful work, no one can be happy. I have never seen it work to the advantage of a child to be left a large sum of money unless the child has participated for many years in the earning of that money and has learned how to use it before receiving it.

While it is wise to be discriminating, the I Ching also cautions that we not allow our hearts to become rigid:

> *Through hardness and selfishness,*
> *the heart grows rigid, and this rigidity*
> *leads to separation from others.*

Seeing someone in need and turning away from him is the beginning of hardness. When someone asks for help and you refuse, selfishly hoarding what you have, the hardness grows. Refusing to forgive someone who has asked for forgiveness is the beginning of rigidity. Soon, you may begin to look at everyone from behind a mask of hardness as a way of protecting yourself from their pleas for help. Your voice may become sharp and your manner truculent, and everyone will avoid you except the hangers-on who are after the few crumbs that fall from your table.

Hardness and selfishness are characteristics of the inferior person. Gentleness and generosity are characteristics of the superior person. Hardness and selfishness, gentleness and generosity each bring their own inevitable results.

Being wealthy also carries with it the obligation not to use wealth to make others feel inadequate or less fortunate than you. Making a show of wealth is one of the surest ways to lose it. Remember that you live in and are part of an aware Universe. To hurt one part of the Universe (someone else) will surely cause a problem for the person who is doing the hurting. If you are the one making the display of wealth, you can be sure that some form of correction will follow. This will not be a correction to hurt or to punish, but to teach. *The Universe will never act against its own best interests, and you are part of the Universe.*

How you use your wealth, therefore, is a balancing act that takes care and discrimination. If you would protect your wealth once you have accumulated it, you must be as cautious as a fox crossing thin ice in your display of wealth and the ways you use it.

You can use the I Ching to seek guidance in matters of wealth in a variety of ways. You can ask:

"What can I expect if I stop accumulating wealth?"

"To what should I turn my attention at this time?"

"What will result if I give money to Harry/Susan?"

"What action should I take with regard to Harry's/ Susan's request for money?"

"What will result for my son/daughter if I leave him/ her my wealth?"

Overcoming Fear and Setting Limits

Once you have accumulated wealth, you must have the wisdom to overcome the fear of losing what you have gained. The I Ching explains:

> *It is only after perfect balance*
> *has been achieved that any*
> *misstep brings imbalance.*

It is only after you have achieved success, wealth, fame, happiness, love, popularity, or possessions that you can then be burdened with the fear of losing them. Thus, the I Ching cautions that you remain modest and vigilant once you have acquired your treasure, whatever it is, or the same law that brought your treasure to you will remove it from you or cause it to work to your detriment.

Modesty will also prevent you from deluding yourself into thinking that your achievements and possessions are the end-all and be-all of life. They are merely the objects you have chosen to lead yourself along the path of life. *It is the path itself that is the end-all and be-all,* for on that path you shall learn the lessons of life and perfect yourself as a divine incarnation.

One of the most important aspects of wealth is knowing when you have enough. A sane person will set limits on the amount of wealth he accumulates. Once you have achieved enough wealth so that you can follow other pursuits, you need not continue putting forth the effort to accumulate wealth.

What stands in the way of setting these bounds is the tendency to keep escalating our standard of living and the gratification of our desires to match or run slightly ahead of our income. This is madness and will keep you on the treadmill for the rest of your life.

Some justify the continued accumulation of wealth by saying, "I like what I do for a living." That may well be, but there are other more important matters to which you should turn your attention once you have accomplished your goal of financial security. What you can do without is oftentimes more important than fulfilling your desires to have more. It is a wise person who knows when he has enough.

It is healthy to set certain bounds for yourself within

which you can experience complete freedom. The I Ching makes this point when it says:

Unlimited possibilities are not suited to us.
If they existed, life would only
dissolve into the boundless.

Who is it that could choose among unlimited possibilities? Just to consider them would take all of eternity. Limitations are troublesome, but they are effective. When you can set limits, you will be able to achieve focus and success and avoid danger. Limit your work, play, wealth gathering, eating, sleeping, and all your activities to their most beneficial limits. Read those words carefully, for in them is a message more precious than the wealth you may seek.

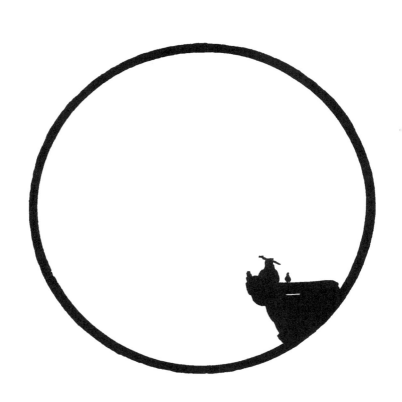

CHAPTER EIGHTEEN

Stillness

In the midst of all activity, there must be a quiet time—a time for contemplation, for meditation, for input from the Universe. Achieving a quiet heart will allow you to be sensitive to the subtle promptings from the world around you. That, in turn, will allow you to move through life effortlessly and smoothly rather than with great effort and blundering.

The I Ching, as we saw in chapter fifteen, counsels us to alternate periods of activity and rest. The following saying from the I Ching also advises us to engage in rest and movement, each at the right time:

> *In order to achieve a quiet heart,*
> *rest and movement must follow each other*
> *in accordance with the demands of the time.*

If you are still when the time for action comes, you will miss your opportunity, and what would have been easy to achieve becomes difficult. If, on the other hand, you are in motion when it is the time for rest, you will be unprepared when the time for action comes. The superior person first achieves a quiet heart and then acts. Whoever acts from these deep levels makes no mistakes and the right action flows naturally. The I Ching wisely instructs:

> *Once you have gained inner mastery*
> *of a problem, it will come about naturally*
> *that the action you take will succeed.*

QUIETING YOUR THOUGHTS

While it is true that you can and do receive information from the Universe in a continuous stream, you can increase and improve your communication by deliberately making time to be quiet, free from interruptions. At the beginning of each of those times, avoid thinking of the things that trouble you, such as worries, family matters, business, money problems, and the like. Instead, remain relaxed and receptive.

During these quiet times, it is good to think about the wisdom of the I Ching. Carrying this book with you and reading one of the sayings is a good way to begin. After that, lightly hold in your mind thoughts about what you have read, and soon the flow of communication from the Universe will begin.

Once you have started the proper flow of communication, the answers to your most pressing questions will come to you. Trust those answers. Remember where the answers are coming from. Remember that you are part of that Source. Remember that the Universe is well inclined, beneficially inclined, that it wants to benefit you (because you are a part of it), and just relax.

If you set aside a time for meditation and find it difficult to quiet your thoughts, don't force yourself in any way. Simply remain calm and gently push the thoughts away, turning your thoughts to one of the bits of wisdom in the I Ching. As the I Ching explains:

In exercises in meditation
and concentration, trying to
force results will lead to an
unwholesome outcome.

Trying to obtain by force that which can only be obtained by relaxation and calmness will produce results opposite from the ones you hope to achieve. By achieving inner composure first, you can develop meditation and concentration naturally, thereby producing the desired result. One of the best ways to gain inner composure is to simply focus your attention on your breath, following it in and out. When you find yourself thinking of something else, gently bring your attention back to your breath. In the beginning, if you can manage five minutes of meditation a day, it will be of great benefit. With this exercise, you can lower your blood pressure, obtain calmness, and find peace.

MODERATION

The way to achieve tranquility is to follow the path of the superior person, who is careful of his words and temperate in eating and drinking. The I Ching says that we can cultivate moderation in our habits through stillness:

Words are movements going from within, outward.
Eating and drinking are movements that go
from without, inward. Both movements
can be modified by tranquility.

Overeating, drinking alcohol, using drugs, incessant talking, and general agitation are all detrimental to achieving stillness, calm, and peace. Everything in its proper measure can benefit you; those same things carried to excess can destroy you.

The I Ching also teaches about the dangers of uncontrolled emotions:

Passion and reason
cannot exist side by side.

Passionate outbursts and uncontrolled fury never lead to stillness. When anger, lust, hatred, or love consumes you, clear, rational thinking is impossible. Such occasions cause great turmoil in your mind, turmoil that may take many hours and even days to subside. It is only when you are able to calmly step back from yourself and "look in" on yourself that true detachment is achieved. That detachment then permits rational thinking, which helps you achieve correct solutions.

Stillness is a great treasure. Being still allows you to perceive the greatness of the Universe. It is through stillness that you can feel your oneness with All-That-Is. Be still.

CHAPTER NINETEEN

Personal Goals

You can succeed, no matter who or what you are. You do not have to be powerful to achieve your goals, nor must you have a strong position in terms of your work or social status. What *is* necessary is that you know the Universal laws that govern the achieving of goals. The I Ching teaches:

> *Even small power, used correctly,*
> *can achieve great success.*

As the above saying reveals, it is not the amount of power with which you begin, but how you use it that creates success. To accomplish a great goal with only a small amount of power is a wonderful accomplishment. It will bring you great respect and allow the power you have to blossom so that you will be able to accomplish other, greater deeds.

To use whatever power you have correctly, consider the following four steps:

First, fix the goal firmly in your mind. See it clearly. Second, imagine yourself attaining it. See the attainment of your goal in as much detail as possible. Third, commit yourself to reaching the goal. True commitment always fulfills itself. There is a great power in commitment. Before you commit yourself, there is always hesitation and uncertainty, but once you fully commit yourself, all your power and drive will come into use without reservation.

Fourth, always use whatever power you have to move in the direction of attainment, taking every opportunity that comes along and turning it to your advantage. Your perseverance must never slacken. Just as dripping water wears away even the hardest rock, you will eventually arrive at your goal. The following saying from the I Ching addresses the importance of using each opportunity to move closer to the attainment of your goal:

Not a whole day.

That saying tells us that when the superior person perceives that action is required, he does not let even a whole day pass before taking the required action. The achievement of your goals requires your complete effort and the complete force of your intention without hesitation. If you are undecided or unsure of your actions, you will be unable to act with your full power.

Boasting Invites Misfortune

Again, in any plan or undertaking that you conceive, your character is of utmost importance. If your character is flawed, if you cannot depend upon yourself to be efficient or careful or cautious or persevering, you are a danger and a detriment to your own plans. The I Ching states:

> *If you are not as you should be,*
> *you will have misfortune, and it does not*
> *further you to undertake anything.*

The path of the inferior person, therefore, is filled with pitfalls of his own making. Even the greatest goal will come to nothing if you have character flaws, but if your character is without flaw, you can carry out even difficult and dangerous undertakings without fear of failure.

Earlier, when I discussed business and wealth, I said that one of the most important character traits to develop is modesty. Modesty will also benefit you immensely on the road to obtaining your personal goals. In another saying that relates to this virtue, the I Ching says:

> *By manifesting a humble attitude,*
> *people will naturally want to help you*
> *and give you good counsel.*

It is part of human nature to love and help the humble and to resent and thwart the arrogant. People soon give up counseling an egotistical person who thinks he knows everything. Every time you depart from modesty, the law of cause and effect will bring you down. It may be gratifying to boast of your achievements, but it always works against you. The I Ching cautions:

Boasting of power, wealth, position,
promotion, success, or influential friends
inevitably invites misfortune and humiliation.

Boasting only confirms that you feel inferior, inadequate, and insecure and that you are trying to add to your stature by boasting. In contrast, the superior person considers that what he has is sufficient and lets it speak for itself. He acts modestly, and in that way assures his continued success. The I Ching also counsels:

At the beginning of a project, if many boastful
claims are made, the successful attainment
of the goal becomes far more difficult.

It is the way of Universal law to bring down the high and uplift the lowly. We can see that law at work in the way mountains are worn down and valleys are filled up. Therefore, before undertaking any serious goal, make no boasts or claims, because they bring resistance from those who hear you. When no claims are put forward, no resistance arises.

If you cultivate modesty, you will make swift, sure progress because no resentment will attach to you. If you remain modest, despite your merit, you will be beloved and will win the support necessary to carry out even difficult and dangerous undertakings. When you make boastful claims, however, you compromise the attainment of your goals. Even if you are moderately successful but have fallen short of your claims, people will say that you failed.

Nurturing the Good

On the way to the achievement of your goals, remember to always strive for that which is highest and best within you. If you want to enjoy the fruits of your goals once you have attained them, you must have attained them in the right way. For instance, there is no taste of real victory if you have cheated to win. Therefore, it is essential that you always polish your already bright virtues. The I Ching teaches:

> *If you neglect your good qualities and virtues,*
> *you will cease to be of value to your friends*
> *and neighbors. Soon, no one will seek*
> *you out or bother about you.*

By nurturing your good qualities and virtues, you ensure that your inner worth will be inexhaustible, and all will seek you out. Like a spring of sparkling, clear water, no matter how much is drawn from you, you still have more. That is true power.

The I Ching makes an important distinction between power and force. Sometimes, when you see a goal in front of you, you are tempted to take it by force, particularly if that is within your capability. The I Ching explains that obtaining anything by force is rarely beneficial in the end:

It is wise and reasonable
not to try to obtain anything by force.

What is obtained by force must be held by force. That constant exertion drains your powers, invites the censure of others, and inevitably leads to regret. It is a law of the Universe that what you obtain by force will ultimately bring you misfortune in one form or another, and a superior person will have none of it. It may appear that something obtained by force is a temporary benefit to the person who obtained it, but in the end, the law will be fulfilled.

On the way to the achievement of your goals, you must also avoid conflict with those with whom you have joined forces to achieve a goal. Even under the best of circumstances, it is difficult to achieve great goals. How much more difficult is it, then, to achieve a goal when you are fighting with your associates? Conflict always weakens. Conflict within a group prevents members of the group from acting as a unit.

Inner conflict is also dangerous. The I Ching tells us:

Conflict within weakens the power
to conquer danger without.

When the time for action has come, inner conflict will cause you to hesitate. Great or dangerous undertakings are to be avoided in times of conflict because achieving success requires a concerted unity of force.

REALISTIC GOALS

During your lifetime, you will achieve many goals—some big, some small—and it is commendable to push yourself to new heights. In addition to the reward of the goal, achieving your goals brings satisfaction and other benefits. There may be praise, for instance, if anyone knows of your achievement or there may be an increase in your own strength, enabling you to reach ever-greater successes.

If, however, you strive to reach unrealistic or unattainable goals, you court disaster and failure, and you may lose even that which you already have. It is good to know when a task is too monumental and to back away. He who takes every turn is not wise. The I Ching teaches:

> *If you attempt too much,*
> *you will end by succeeding in nothing.*

The superior person, therefore, does not overreach himself or strive foolishly. In that way, he enjoys a lifetime of success.

CHAPTER TWENTY

Words, Deeds, and Intent

All actions are the blossoms of thought. Even those actions that you think are spontaneous have been earlier decided in your mind. Whether your actions bring you good fortune or ill fortune is *entirely* dependent upon your intentions in carrying out the actions.

All words and deeds spring from within. If your heart is pure and your motivations are those of the superior person, your words will be direct and powerful, and your actions will produce far-reaching, beneficial effects. If your heart is not as it should be, can anything else happen but that you will fall into a pit of your own creation? Therefore, take care in what you say and do, for by your words and deeds you create good fortune and misfortune.

The I Ching notes the extraordinary power of words and deeds:

> *Through words and deeds,*
> *the superior person moves heaven and earth.*

If you want to benefit yourself as much as possible, you will see to it that you always intend to benefit everyone and everything as much as possible. Natural law will then take care of the rest, bringing you inestimable benefits.

OUR FEELINGS SEND US MESSAGES

Listen to your conscience. Your conscience is there to protect you. It is built into you from the beginning. It is patterned after what is right in the Universe. When you act or think about acting, you unconsciously compare your intended action to the Universal pattern of perfection in your mind. Then you form a judgment—and act.

Sometimes you may act contrary to what you know to be right, believing you are benefiting yourself. If you have received what you believe to be a temporary benefit by acting against what you know to be right action, you may unconsciously or consciously decide to follow that new pattern the next time a similar situation arises. That is when the Universe steps in to help you correct your course.

It is true that you are a divine incarnation, a perfect being, but when you act out of greed, selfishness, meanness, hatred, or other such inferior motives, you act the part of a lesser being. To help you stay on the path of the superior person, the Universe always shows you that by acting against what you know to be right, you will, in the end, incur misfortune. That misfortune is meant to inform you that your actions were not as they should have been. In other words, the feelings of pain, despair, and frustration that you experience are there to let you know that you have departed from the path of the superior person. Feelings of love and joy let you know that you are on the correct path.

Whatever you are experiencing is a result of your intentions, your thoughts, and your actions. It is you who are in charge of your fate, not another. The I Ching explains:

> *You have received a nature that is innately good.*
> *When your thoughts and actions are in accord*
> *with your nature, you will enjoy great*
> *good fortune and supreme success.*

The I Ching also acknowledges that you may, from time to time, stray and thus the ancient text wisely counsels:

> *On the path of the superior person,*
> *there are always digressions, but you must*
> *turn back before going too far.*

HATRED BINDS

The wisdom of the I Ching warns of the tyranny of hatred. Hatred can consume you if you indulge yourself in such passion. Sometimes you may use the word *hatred* casually. For instance, you may say, "I hate the taste of castor oil." What you mean is that you intensely dislike the taste of castor oil. I am not talking about sentiments like that. I am speaking of the hatred you feel for people and sometimes animals that have harmed you in some way or the hatred you feel for places where you have experienced great harm.

The effects you experience in your body when you feel hatred are exceptionally detrimental to you. Adrenaline pulses through your veins. You secrete all kinds of chemicals that the body produces in response to your hate, chemicals that destroy your body, put lines in your face, and ruin the quality of life. The I Ching counsels:

Do not hate.
Hatred is a form of subjective involvement
that binds you to the hated object.

Hatred is a product of evil, and to the extent that you allow yourself to feel hatred, you become an instrument of that evil. Not only that, but when you hate someone, you draw that person to you. Is that what you want? To eliminate the connection, you only need to dismiss the person from your thoughts. To combat evil, respond with goodness.

When we feel hatred, we often wish that the person we hate would disappear from our lives. That can essentially happen when you dismiss that person from your thoughts. When a person is not in your thoughts, it is as if he or she *has* disappeared. To dismiss someone from your thoughts means that you consciously stop thinking about that person and replace your thoughts about that person with other thoughts. In other words, you think about something else. You may have to do that many times before thoughts of the person stop recurring in your mind, but be assured that eventually those thoughts will stop and you will then be free from the tyranny of your hatred.

Sometimes you may feel hatred for another person because you have been told that the person has said bad things about you. In such cases, you still have control over what takes place. The I Ching teaches:

> *Slander will be silenced if you do not*
> *gratify it with injured retorts.*

You can spend a lifetime tracking down and defending yourself against the negative things people say. It is better to simply go on with your own affairs. With nothing to keep the talk alive, it will die for lack of attention. The best defense against slander is to live the life of the superior person, letting your actions and conduct speak for you.

THE FOUR RESTRAINTS

You always have a choice about how to respond to events—if you are in control of your responses. When you allow yourself to react on the basis of your emotions rather than your good judgment, you forfeit your choice. The I Ching describes this situation in the following saying:

*To act on the spur of every caprice,
ultimately leads to humiliation.*

What the heart desires, we tend to run after without a moment's hesitation. There are four restraints that are wise to consider before acting or reacting. These restraints can free you from unwanted ties to people or events.

First, do not run precipitately after all persons you would like to influence. Instead, hold back if it is unseemly to make an approach. For instance, if you know of someone with whom you would like to have a relationship, it might not be the right action to go, unintroduced, to that person and try to strike up a relationship. It might be better to go to someone you know who is close to that person and ask that person to introduce you to his friend.

Second, do not yield to every whim of those who are engaging you in their service. If an employer asks you to do something that would be morally incorrect for you, you will be benefited if you refuse on the grounds that you do not feel right in granting the request. If the person is well-meaning, he or she will respect you for your action.

Third, where the moods of the heart are concerned, do not ignore the possibility of inhibition, for this is the basis of human freedom. In other words, even in the face of desires that may strongly pull you, develop the strength to choose the wise course of action. This can be difficult, but it is essential if you are to be in charge of your fate, and such restraint leads to great success and good fortune.

Fourth, do not act on the impulse or whim of every emotion. Think things through before taking actions for which you may later feel regret.

Gaining Inspiration from Worthy Heroes

An excellent way to achieve the goal of correct thoughts, actions, and reactions is to read about great deeds that have been done in the past and great sayings that have been handed down through the centuries. In that way, you will gain inspiration from worthy heroes, which will help you in walking the path of the superior person. The I Ching encourages us to study the deeds and sayings of the great ones:

A superior person acquaints himself with many sayings of antiquity and many deeds of the past and thus strengthens his character.

By studying the sayings that have survived the test of the centuries, you gain wisdom. By learning about the deeds of the ancient heroes, you gain inspiration. Wisdom, coupled with inspiration, leads to great good fortune and supreme success.

CHAPTER TWENTY-ONE

Death

Death is a transition. It is part of the flow of life. To become small, something must first be big. To become big, something must first be small. To become cold, something must first be hot. To become hot, something must first be cold. To become dead, something must first be alive. To become alive, something must first be dead.

Everything comes from its opposite. If life and death did not follow that alternating pattern, they would be the only things in the Universe that did not. The coming and going of life and death mirror the ebb and flow of the oceans, the waxing and waning of the moon, and all else in the Universe.

It is the alternation of life and death that, like varying tones of music, gives harmony and beauty to existence. In the Universe and in nature, without the passing away of the old and the birth of the new, life would become a bore. Not only that, it is death that gives life its meaning.

A person of true understanding is secure in the knowledge that all is one. He experiences himself to be as much a part of the Universe as the stars and the trees, to be as enduring as All-That-Is. Knowing that time is only an illusion, he feels no break with time. The I Ching says of this kind of person:

> *To a person of true understanding,*
> *it makes no difference whether*
> *death comes early or late.*

A person of true understanding cultivates himself and uses his time productively. His sense of the transitory nature of life does not impel him to uninhibited revelry so that he can enjoy life while it lasts. Nor does it impel him to yield to melancholy and sadness, thereby spoiling the time remaining to him.

An Endless Progression

Understanding your oneness with the Universe, you need have no fear of the moment of death, which is only a point of transition. It is like walking through a doorway from one room into another and no more remarkable than any other moment.

It is unworthy of us to believe that our magnificent Universe, which contains such beauty and grandeur, would crown the ending of our lives with emptiness. Just observing nature and the constant changing of the seasons shows us that death is part of life, that they go together, like winter and spring, that one is an extension of the other and that both are a part of the One.

That is the way: an endless progression, not toward perfection but *through* perfection. Everything is always perfect. It is a state from which you cannot depart. The Universe is not flawed in any way. Relax. Be of good cheer. You have all of eternity within which to exist.

CHAPTER TWENTY-TWO

The Superior Person

Throughout the I Ching and this book, there are many references to "the superior person." As I said at the beginning of this book, the term refers to a person who acts with worthy motives, who strives to be the best person possible. Being that type of person brings the greatest rewards imaginable.

The I Ching says:

> *Every person must have*
> *something to follow, a lodestar.*

We all need something to bring out the best in ourselves and to provide direction for our development. By holding the image of the superior person in your mind as your lodestar, you will achieve not only supreme success but also great happiness.

To know the qualities of the superior person is of great benefit. I have listed a few of them on the following pages.

He is humble.

He is willing to let others go ahead of him.

He is courteous.

His good manners stem from his humility and concern for others.

He is good-natured.

He is calm.

He is always inwardly acknowledging the wonder he feels for all of creation.

He is willing to give another the credit.

He speaks well of everyone, ill of no one.

He believes in himself and in others.

He does not swear.

He is physically fit.

He does not overindulge.

He knows what is enough.

He can cheerfully do without.

He is willing to look within himself to find the error.

He is true to what he believes.

He is gentle.

He is able to make decisions and to act on them.

He is reverent.

He carries on his teaching activity.

He does not criticize or find fault.

He is willing to take the blame.

He does not have to prove anything.

He is content within himself.

He is dependable.

He is aware of danger.

He is certain of his right to be here.

He is certain of your right to be here.

He is aware that the Universe is unfolding as it should.

He is generally happy.

He laughs easily.

He can cry.

It is all right with him if another wins.

His happiness for another's happiness is sincere.

His sorrow for another's sorrow is sincere.

He has no hidden agendas.

He is thrifty and therefore is not in want.

He finds a use for everything.

He honors everyone and is, therefore, honored.

He pays attention to detail.

He is conscientious.

He values everyone, and therefore everyone values him.

He is optimistic

He is trustworthy.

He is good at salvage.

He is patient.

He knows the value of silence.

He is peaceful.

He is generous.

He is considerate.

He is fair.

He is courageous in the face of fear.

He is clean.

He is tidy.

He does not shirk his duties.

He causes others to feel special.

He expects things to turn out well.

He is always seeking to benefit others in some way.

His presence has a calming effect.

He is not attached to things.

He sees obstruction as opportunity.

He sees opposition as a signpost deflecting him in the right direction.

He sets a good example.

He is joyous of heart.

He takes thought for the future.

He wastes nothing; therefore he always has enough.

He has good manners.

He obtains nothing by force.

He overlooks the mistakes of others.

He has greatness of spirit.

He is clearheaded.

He does more than his share.

He meets others more than halfway.

He rests when it is time to rest; he acts when it is time to act.

He feels no bitterness.

He is forgiving.

He does not pretend.

He is not cynical.

He studies.

He reveres the ancient masters.

He is inspiring.

He nourishes nature and is, therefore, nourished by nature.

He leaves things better than he found them.

He does not make a show.

He practices goodness.

He is simple.

His intentions are always beneficial.

He is a wellspring of determination.

He does not boast.

He produces long-lasting effects.

He has endurance.

He is flexible in his thinking.

He does not overreach himself.

He does not overspend himself.

He does not strive foolishly.

He is consistent.

He does not go into debt.

He lives a simple life.

He nurtures his good qualities and virtues.

He is sensitive to his inner promptings.

He exists in the present.

He feels no break with time.

He is cautious.

He is kind.

He holds his goals lightly in his mind, allows no opposing thoughts to enter and, as a result of natural law, is drawn inexorably to his goals.

He seeks enlightenment.

He sets limitations for himself within which he experiences complete freedom.

He is careful of his words, knowing he is reflected in them.

He does not use flattery.

He depends on himself for his happiness.

He feels secure.

He knows the truth of his existence.

He does not strive for wealth, fame, popularity, or possessions.

He does not complain.

He turns back immediately if he discovers that he has strayed from the path of the superior person.

He practices daily self-renewal of his character.

The Daily Self-Renewing of Character

It takes Herculean effort to reach the peak of perfection in any area of life and continuous effort to remain there. That is also true for living an I Ching life—a life lived in harmony with the ways of the Universe, a life that allows you to naturally express your authentic self. The I Ching tells us:

*Only through daily self-renewal of character
can you continue at the height of your powers.*

Every day you must expend some effort in refreshing yourself through the ways of the superior person. Reading the I Ching or other great books, talking to like-minded people, teaching others, studying the deeds of ancient heroes, and thinking about your actions of the day to see whether you are being the best that you can be are all ways to continue on the path. As you grow in awareness, your power will grow and your attainments will be like the harvest after a perfect summer. There is no other activity that will reward you as richly as the daily self-renewing of your character.

Leave Taking

This is where I leave you, my friend. I am not leaving you in any real sense of the word, for there is no place to go. We are here, all of us, eternally. And we are all one. Separation, in the Universal sense of the word, is an illusion. When each of us comes to know that, we will all act in everyone's best interests.

Remember that you are a divine child of an eternal Universe, as much a part of the Universe as the Universe itself. May you learn quickly, benefit greatly, and attain to sublime wisdom. May you experience great good fortune, *and may you mount to the skies of success as though on the wings of six dragons!*

Index